INDIAN COUNTRY
by MEIC POVEY

sgriptcymru
contemporarydramawales

INDIAN COUNTRY
Copyright © Meic Povey 2003

All rights Reserved

No part of this book may be reproduced in any form,
by photocopying or by any electronical means,
including information storage of retrieval systems,
without permission in writing from both the copyright
owner and the publisher of this book

INDIAN COUNTRY
by MEIC POVEY

sgriptcymru
contemporarydrama**wales**

presents the premiere of

INDIAN COUNTRY

by Meic Povey

First performed at Chapter, 31 April 2003

Note: Text was correct at time of going to press,
but may have changed during rehearsal.

[ ] bracketed text was cut during rehearsals.

sgriptcymru is the national new writing company for Wales, working in both Welsh and English.

Our mission is to discover, develop and produce the best possible work of contemporary Welsh and Wales-based playwrights. We aim to present theatre that is exciting, passionate, fresh and distinctive: to reflect the concerns of twenty-first century Wales to audiences, at home and beyond, through a commitment to theatre of the highest possible standards.

As both development agency and producing company **sgript**cymru has the responsibility to encourage and support playwrights across the length and breadth of Wales. For example, through our Wales-wide development work and a rolling programme of workshops – **sgript**saturday – we aim to uncover the next generation of Welsh dramatists. We also offer a free reading service to all writers who send us a play, including written reports from our team of experienced readers, which may lead to a commission or other development through readings.

". . . **testament to the strength of writing in Wales and the vision of Sgript Cymru,**" The Big Issue Cymru, May 2001

Since its inception in 2000, **sgript**cymru has gained an enviable reputation as an exciting and fast-growing component of the new writing scene in Great Britain. To date, these are the company's productions:

Yr Hen Blant	by Meic Povey, which opened at The National Eisteddfod in 2000
Art and Guff	by Catherine Tregenna (in association with Soho Theatre Co.)
Crazy Gary's Mobile Disco	
	by Gary Owen (co–production with Paines Plough.)
Mab	by Sera Moore-Williams (co-production with Y Gymraes)
Ysbryd Beca	by Geraint Lewis
Franco's Bastard	by Dic Edwards (Best New Play – TiW awards 2002)
Dosbarth	by Geraint Lewis (the Commissioned Play for the 2002 National Eisteddfod)
past away	by first time playwright Tracy Harris
Diwrnod Dwynwen	6 short plays by Fflur Dafydd, Angharad Devonald, Angharad Elen, Meleri Wyn James, Dafydd Llewelyn, Nia Roberts

sgriptcymru – The Company:

Artistic Director:	Simon Harris
Administrative Director:	Mai Jones
Development Director:	Bill Hopkinson
Associate Director:	Elen Bowman
Literary Manager:	Caron Wyn Edwards
Marketing Officer:	Siân Melangell Dafydd
Artistic Associate:	Bethan Jones
Marketing Consultant:	Stephan Stockton the next step 02920 667 989
Graphic Designer:	Neil Wallace, A1
Web Designer:	Martin Rowlinson
Photographer:	Image: Siân Trenberth
	Brian Tarr
	production: Huw Talfryn Walters

sgriptcymru – Board of Directors:

Ann Beynon (chair), David Clarke, Philippa Davies, Mark Drakeford, Nicola Heywood-Thomas, Richard Houdmont, Elwyn Tudno Jones, David Seligman, Paul Islwyn Thomas, Elinor Williams, Mared Hughes (associate member).

mailing list: If you would like to be on the **sgript**cymru free mailing list please send your details to:

> **sgript**cymru,
> Chapter, Heol y Farchnad, Treganna, Caerdydd, CF5 1QE
> Chapter, Market Road, Canton, Cardiff, CF5 1QE

T: 029 2023 6650
sgriptcymru@sgriptcymru.com
www.sgriptcymru.com

sgriptcymru is a registered charity no: 702117

This production is supported by:
> Arts Council of Wales, WDA, Cardiff 2008.

With thanks to:
> Åsa Malmsten
> W.N.O.
> Museum of Welsh Life

the next production by sgriptcymru

The acclaimed novel and television series, **Amdani**, becomes a new stage play on tour in Wales and in London this Autumn.

A women's rugby team create their own battles in this large-scale Welsh-language tour of **Amdani** by Bethan Gwanas. The original novel, described as 'the first Welsh novel to deal with sex openly and naturally from a woman's perspective' follows the life of a feisty woman named Llinos. She overcomes a difficult marriage to her husband, Wayne, by galvanising the local women into forming a successful rugby team, despite the hostility of their men, and strong opposition from that bastion of masculinity – the local rugby club.

Bethan Gwanas is an acclaimed writer, well-known for her award-winning books for young people, including **Amdani** and a best-selling novel for young Welsh learners, **Llinyn Trons** (Pants String).

The fun and realism, strong female characters and deep contemporary insight into the dynamics of intimate lives mark out **Amdani** as a breakthrough work in recent times.

www.amdani.co.uk

sgriptcymru
contemporarydramawales
Chapter, Heol y Farchnad, Caerdydd, CF5 1QE / Chapter, Market Road, Cardiff, CF5 1QE
029 2023 6650   sgriptcymru@sgriptcymru.com   www.sgriptcymru.com

WRITER: Meic Povey

Meic started his professional career as an actor with Cwmni Theatr Cymru in 1968, but has been a freelance writer for over thirty years. One of Wales' most prolific playwrights, he is generally regarded as one of the leading dramatists Wales has produced. His work for the theatre, television and film include: *Nos Sadwrn Bach*, *Aelwyd Gartrefol*, *Taff Acre*, *Meistres y Chwarae*, *Camau Troellog*, *Sul y Blodau*, *Deryn*, *Babylon By-Passed*, *Y Filltir Sgwâr*, *Christmas Story*, *Nel*, *Yr Ynys*, *Terfyn*, *Y Cadfridog*, *Chwara Plant*, *Gwaed Oer*, *Diwedd Y Byd*, *Yn Debyg Iawn i Ti a Fi*, *Y Weithred*, *Wyneb Yn Wyneb*, *Perthyn*, *Fel Anifail*, *Yr Heliwr*, *Bonansa!*, *Tair*, *Talcen Caled*, *Yr Hen Blant*. Most recently, his work includes *Sylw* (Royal Welsh College of Music and Drama in association with **sgript**cymru, 2001), and the eagerly awaited *Bob a'i Fam*, which will be shown on S4C later in the year. An English translation of Meic's play *Tair* was recently presented by **sgript**cymru at The Traverse Theatre in Edinburgh and, as part of a prestigious new European collaboration, has been planned for translation and production into several major European languages through a **sgript**cymru partnership with The Royal Shakespeare Company. *Indian Country* is his first English-language stage play.

DIRECTOR: Simon Harris

Simon Harris is Artistic Director of **sgript**cymru and *Indian Country* will be his third production for the company. Born and brought up in Swansea, Simon studied English at University College, London and trained as an actor at RADA. He founded Thin Language Theatre Company in 1992, directing *Forever Yours Marie Lou* and *Nothing To Pay* for the company, which he also adapted from the novel by Caradoc Evans. Other directorial work includes *The Dresser* at Plymouth Theatre Royal. As a writer, his first play *Badfinger*, premiered at The Donmar Warehouse and was nominated in the 1997 Evening Standard Drama Awards. His previous productions for **sgript**cymru include *Franco's Bastard* by Dic Edwards (Best New Play – TiW awards 2002) and most recently, *past away* by Tracy Harris, which opened at Chapter Arts Centre, Cardiff, before touring across Wales as well as to Bradford's Theatre in the Mill and Jackson's Lane Theatre in London.

Gregg: Stuart Laing

Stuart trained at the Drama Centre in London. His theatre credits include *Games Room, Billy & the Crab Lady,* and *Food for Thought* for Soho Theatre, Jonathan Harvey's *Hushabye Mountain* for English Touring Theatre (Hampstead Theatre and National Tour). He played the character Molina in *Kiss of the Spiderwoman* at Leicester Haymarket; *Trouble with Girls* at the National Theatre Studio. Other credits include *Over Hear* at Bristol's Old Vic, *Salt Lake Psycho,* Man in the Moon Theatre, *Loot* at Thorndike Theatre and *Bad Company* at The Bush.

TV includes: *Cambridge Spies, Murphy's Law, Burn It, In a Land of Plenty, Kavannah QC, Blood and Peaches, Devil's Advocate, In Your Dreams, Bedhead, Minder, Bob Martin* and *Berkeley Square.* Films include: *The Lawless Heart, Butterfly Man, South West Nine, The Truth Game, Strong Language, Gaston's War* and *Three Steps to Heaven.*

Young Mos: Sion Pritchard

Sion was born and bred in Gwynedd. He moved to Cardiff two years ago to train as an actor at the Royal Welsh College of Music and Drama, where he is currently midway through his training.

His professional work includes *Pen Tennyn.* He also recently performed in Fuccechio, Italy as part of a performance/montage of Buchner's *Woyzeck* for Elan Wales directed by Firenza Guidi.

Sion is excited about working with **sgript**cymru as a growing Welsh company. He is also proud of working on a piece written by Meic Povey as he is Sion's favourite Welsh playwright and is also from the same area.

Old Mos: Rhys Richards

Rhys' theatre credits include an Interlude: *Y Mawr, y Bach a'r Llai Fyth* with Cwmni Cyfri Tri; *Fala Aurion Bach* with Theatr Crwban; *Lewis Jones,* Theatrig; *Iechyd Da,* Theatr Bara Caws; *Y Cylch Sialc* and *Druid's Rest,* both with Theatr Gwynedd. Film and television credits include *Pengelli, A55, Pen Tennyn, C'Mon Midffild, Iechyd Da, Cylch Gwaed,* for which he won Best Actor with Bafta Cymru in 1993, *Y Wisg Sidan, Treflan, Pum Cynnig i Gymro/Bride of War, Eldra,* and *Yr Heliwr/Mind to Kill.*

Gwyneth/Elin: Eiry Thomas

Eiry is from Cardiff and trained at Rose Bruford College. This is her first appearance with **sgrip**cymru. Her theatre credits include: *Skylight* for Theatre West Glamorgan, *Her Big Chance* (Talking Heads), *The Elves and the Shoemakers, Romeo and Juliet, A Taste of Honey, 101 Dalmatians, Under Milk Wood, Fern Hill* (all for the Sherman Theatre Co., Cardiff); *Calon Ci* and *'i'* for Dalier Sylw.
Television appearances include: *The Bench* (2 series), *Tair Stori, JARA, A Mind to Kill, Gary Phelps, Safe House*.
Radio work includes *Station Road, King of Bath, Just So Stories, Pembroke Arcadia, Fishermen of Black Tar, Island of the Blessed, Skipping for Toffee, One Good Turn, Couple of the Year.*
She is married and has one son, Gruffudd.

DESIGNER: John Howes

John trained at Motley Theatre Design Course and by now works both as a Theatre Designer and Production Designer/ Art Director for film and television. Recent theatre includes *Home* by Talia Theatre and *Uncle Vanya* for Subaru Theatre Company, Tokyo. Recent Film/TV includes *Dal Yma/Nawr* by Fiction Factory for S4C, *First Degree* for BBC Wales and, as Production Designer, *Alone in the Dark* for Metropolis International Pictures.

LIGHTING DESIGNER: Elanor Higgins

Elanor is a freelance Lighting Designer living in Cardiff. She has been working as a part-time lecturer at the Royal Welsh College of Music and Drama for two years, at which she was previously a student.
Her lighting work for **sgript**cymru includes *Diwrnod Dwynwen, Dosbarth, past away, Franco's Bastard, Ysbryd Beca, Art and Guff* and *Yr Hen Blant*. She has also worked on *Articulate* (Dawns Rubicon), *The Caretaker* (Torch Theatre), *Erogenous Zones* (Sherman Theatre), *Diwedd y Byd* (Theatr Gwynedd), *Radio Cymru, Perthyn, Wyneb yn Wyneb, Y Madogwys* and *Tair* (Dalier Sylw), *Rats, Buckets and Bombs* (Nottingham Playhouse). She has also worked as a full-time lighting technician for the Welsh National Opera, the Royal National Theatre and The Haymarket Theatre, Leicester.

STAGE MANAGER: Lisa Skelding

Lisa graduated from the Royal Welsh College of Music and Drama in 1998 where she studied Stage Management. She began her career as part of a producing team with television companies such as Bracan, Boda and more recently, Alfresco, on its production of *Treflan*. Her theatre work includes past productions for **sgript**cymru, *Diwrnod Dwynwen, Ysbryd Beca* and *past away*, and she spent a period recently with Cwmni Mega, on the play *Perthyn*.

STAGE MANAGEMENT: Ryan Evans
Ryan has recently graduated from the Royal Welsh College of Music and Drama as a Stage Manager; he has recently worked as Production Manager on *Speakeasy* with Michael Bogdanov, and has worked on other productions including *One Flew Over The Cuckoo's Nest* at The Torch Theatre, *Sylw* by Meic Povey and *Cegin y Diafol* by Sion Eirian. During his time at college he spent nine months in New York working at a theatre camp. A Porthcawl lad, he hopes to develop his professional career by working in Welsh Theatre.

COMPOSER: Dyfan Jones
Dyfan returned to live in Aberdare after studying in London in the early 90s. He has been working extensively in Wales and further afield ever since.
His theatre work includes *Bonansa!*, *Radio Cymru*, *Y Cinio* and *Language of Heaven*, amongst others, for Dalier Sylw; *Cider with Rosie*, *Ac Abertawe'n Fflam*, *Cylchdroi*, *20/20*, *Codi Stêm*, *Spam Man*, *Skylight*, *I'r Byw* and *Nia Ben Aur* for na n'Óg Theatre; *Rape of the Fair Country*, *House of Rebecca*, *Song of Faith*, *Abigail's Party*, *To Kill a Mockingbird* and *Oh What a Lovely War* for Clwyd Theatr Cymru.
His credits in the television, film and orchestral medias include *Iechyd Da* (series 1–6), *Pam Fi Duw* (series 1–6), *Monologues*, *Pobol y Cwm* (film), *31/12/99*, *Bydd yn Wrol*, *Hi-Line* and *Rumble in the Jungle* (Scottish National Orchestra), *JARA*, *Dreaming of Joseph Lees*, *Hotel Eddie* and *Fel Ci a Cath*.
Dyfan is pleased to be working with **sgript**cymru.

ASSISTANT DIRECTOR: Sara Lloyd
Originally from Anglesey, North Wales, Sara graduated in Philosophy from Cardiff University and then trained at Royal Welsh College of Music and Drama. As an actress, Sara's theatre work includes *Flora's War* (Clwyd Theatr Cymru), *Dosbarth* (**sgript**cymru), *A Taste of Honey* and *Sweetheart* (Salisbury Playhouse). Her television credits include *Hearts of Gold* (BBC), *Treflan* (Alfresco), *Tipyn o Stâd* (Ffilmiau Eryri), *Bad Girls* (ITV), and *Salidas* (Ffilmiau'r Nant).
As a Director, Sara has assisted on *The Nest* for Living Pictures and *Diwrnod Dwynwen* for **sgript**cymru, both with Elen Bowman.

INDIAN COUNTRY

by MEIC POVEY

CHARACTERS:

        GREGG

        GWYNETH / ELIN

        YOUNG MOS

        OLD MOS

TIME: SUMMER, 1958 / PRESENT TIME

PLACE: ERYRI (SNOWDONIA), NORTH WALES

A SPACE.
A SMALL LIGHT COMES UP ON **OLD MOS,** FIFTY NINE YEARS OLD. HE IS STANDING IN A BLEAK, DESOLATE PLACE, WITH THE THIN, CRUEL WIND ABOUT HIS EARS. HE IS AT HIS MOTHER'S FUNERAL **(GWYNETH)** IN THE PRESENT TIME. HE REMAINS IN HIS BLACK, FUNERAL ATTIRE THROUGHOUT THE PLAY, AND IN THE PRESENT TIME.

HE IS STILL, AND FOR THE MOST PART, EXPRESSIONLESS. HE STANDS SILENT FOR A WHILE; THEN HE BRINGS TO VIEW A JAPANESE HANDGUN (CIRCA SECOND WORLD WAR). HE CONSIDERS IT HARD; HE BRINGS IT UP TO CHEST LEVEL. THERE IS NO OBVIOUS GESTURE, BUT ENOUGH TO GENERATE CURIOSITY AS TO WHAT HIS INTENTIONS ARE. EVENTUALLY, HIS ARM (AND GUN) DROPS TO THE SIDE.

HE DOES NOT ADDRESS THE AUDIENCE DIRECTLY; HE IS REMEMBERING, AND MAKING SENSE OF THINGS.

OLD MOS: From the moment they lowered him
into the deep soil
She knew
She knew, that whatever else happened along her not altogether insignificant journey
She would return
Even if she rode to London to see the Queen
And sat in palaces drinking the finest tea
Speaking of a land and time when only one tongue was spoken
She would return
From the moment she threw the first fistful of dirt against the polished lid, and heard its echo ringing down the long years
She knew, that like my father she'd only have that single bit of wood to protect her from the sudden downpour.
Whatever else, she would return to this one same spot, for the last dance
Mr. and Mrs. Parry.

HE CARESSES THE HANDGUN

>   Why wait, I say
>   Why drum my fingers for, what, another ten or twenty?
>   When I know in heart that I must also return
>   Rest not your shovels, lads
>   One more for luck
>   'And son'.

HE CONSIDERS

>   Not yet, perhaps
>   Better to make sense of it all
>   Someone might ask on the other side
>   Don't leave ignorant.

THE LIGHT CHANGES SLIGHTLY, IN ORDER TO CONVEY A CHANGE OF MOOD

>   *Run . . . I said*
>   *Hurry, mam!*
>   *The bracken's ten feet tall and full of Apache!*
>   *Wait . . . she said*
>   *Look at the men in black, come to take your father home*
>   *A young life, too brave for his own good*
>   *Closer: they've decked him out in green pyjamas; he looks serene*
>   *No! Let's take the horse and go; let's climb higher!*
>   *Let's stay on the mountain, always.*
>   *Not always*
>   *Look at the men in black*
>   *I won't be here forever . . . she said.*
>   (PAUSE)
>   Who cares about death, when two lorries from Boreham Wood, somewhere in England, carrying the great wall of

China, are stuck on Aberglaslyn Bridge?
Who cares, when all the fun is watching strangers trying to reverse, and knowing that reversing is totally alien to them?
Beats a funeral, any day!

THE LIGHT CHANGES. IN THE CHANGE, **YOUNG MOS** HAS APPEARED, THIRTEEN, GOING ON FOURTEEN. HE INHABITS THE WORLD OF **1958**. HE IS DONE UP AS A COWBOY, IN MAINLY HOME-MADE GARB. HE HAS TWO GUNS – A TOY, FIRING CAPS, AND A WOODEN ONE. OLD MOS DOES NOT DIRECTLY LOOK AT HIM – BUT WE SENSE THEY ARE ONE AND THE SAME

YOUNG MOS: The bracken's ten feet tall and full of Apache!

THE LIGHT FADES ON OLD AND YOUNG MOS.
GREGG GROSVENOR, A JADED AMERICAN OF FORTY YEARS APPEARS WITH A RUCKSACK SLUNG OVER HIS BACK. HE SETTLES, AND PENSIVELY ENJOYS THE PANORAMIC VIEW.

GREGG: Another day; another dollar . . .

HE BECOMES MILDLY INTERESTED IN THE SOUND OF A SMALL AIRCRAFT – FAINT AT FIRST BUT THEN APPROACHING, THEN OVERHEAD BEFORE FINALLY FADING. FROM HIS RUCKSACK, HE GETS OUT A HALF BOTTLE OF WHISKEY (ALMOST FULL), AND A PORNOGRAPHIC MAGAZINE. HE TAKES A COUPLE OF SLUGS FROM THE FORMER, AND FLICKS IDLY THROUGH THE LATTER, BEFORE RETURNING BOTH TO THE RUCKSACK. THERE IS A TINNY 'BANG'; GREGG IS STARTLED. YOUNG MOS APPEARS. HE CIRCLES GREGG, FIRING THE TOY GUN, WHILE GREGG LOOKS ON, UNIMPRESSED.

GREGG: (FINALLY) So who the fuck are you meant to be?

YOUNG MOS: (VISIBLY SHAKEN) Ch . . . charlie!
No! Mos, really! Charlie . . . is somebody else! (HE PAUSES) 'You American?

GREGG:	No, I'm an alien. My flying saucer's just beyond the pass.
YOUNG MOS:	(IN 'CHARACTER') Stick 'em up! (HE PAUSES) 'You with the film?
GREGG:	Who's Charlie?
YOUNG MOS:	Pretty's friend!
GREGG:	Who . . !
YOUNG MOS:	I'm Charlie . . . and Alwyn Fedw, he's Pretty. He's a cowboy too!
GREGG:	Right.
YOUNG MOS:	**Are** you with the film? **I** want to be a film star!
GREGG:	You do?
YOUNG MOS:	Just like Ingrid Bergman!
GREGG:	She was a woman, last time I looked.
YOUNG MOS:	Do you know her? I've seen her passing in the big, black car!
GREGG:	Know her? I know 'em all.
YOUNG MOS:	Are you a star? I've never seen you in the Neuadd in Pendryn.
GREGG:	The 'what' in the 'where' . . !
YOUNG MOS:	*Pictiws!* I mean . . . the pictures.

GREGG: You aint been goin' to the right movies, kid. 'Bad Day At Black Rock' – 'seen that? I'm one of the bad guys. I've always played bad guys . . .

YOUNG MOS: Who's the good guy?

GREGG: Spence. Spencer Tracy, pal of mine from way back.

YOUNG MOS: *Esgob!* (Goodness!) Really?

GREGG: (REMEMBERING; TRUTHFULLY) Really. It was easy then.

YOUNG MOS: Are you a star in the film here?

GREGG: What . . .? (HE PAUSES; AND JUST FOR THE HELL OF IT): Uh . . . no. I'm the director.

YOUNG MOS: No, you're not! Unless . . . your name is Mark Robson.

GREGG: (RECOVERING) Well, not **the** director, obviously! Hell, would I be talking to you?

YOUNG MOS: What are you then?

GREGG: (MILDLY INTROSPECTIVELY) What am I. (RECOVERING) What am I? I assist.

YOUNG MOS: Assist?

GREGG: That's correct. As in 'assistant'. I get things done. I make 'em sleep at night!

YOUNG MOS: Have you been building the great wall of Yangcheng?

GREGG: Today? Uh . . . no. 'Late getting up.

YOUNG MOS: The plaster sheets came all the way from England somewhere, but the lorries were too big to turn on Aberglaslyn Bridge and got stuck!

YOUNG MOS LAUGHS AT THE MEMORY.

GREGG: That's funny?

YOUNG MOS: They tried to reverse, but couldn't! The English can't go back!

ANOTHER FIT OF LAUGHTER. GREGG SMILES.

GREGG: So what happened . . ?

YOUNG MOS: They went to see Dafydd Bach; he can drive anything!

GREGG: I'm not on the wall. I told you, I assist. Y'know . . . the director?

YOUNG MOS: Mark Robson!

GREGG: He wouldn't be where he is today without me!

YOUNG MOS: Is Ingrid Bergman nice?

GREGG: Think pie.

YOUNG MOS: Can I see her?

GREGG: Pay your ten cents, like the rest.

YOUNG MOS: I've seen her passing in the big, black car!

GREGG: That's twice.

YOUNG MOS: Alwyn Fedw – he's my best friend – he says that Miss Bergman said 'hello' to him in Eirlys Tan Rhiw's shop, but I don't believe him because . . . because he's a liar!

GREGG: Your best friend? That's terrible!

YOUNG MOS: Yes, a liar. And anyway, Miss Bergman would never go to Eirlys Tan Rhiw's shop because . . . because it's not rich enough!

GREGG: Uh-huh.

YOUNG MOS: Eirwen Wilias – she's our Sunday school teacher – has been telling us all about it!

GREGG: Let me get this straight: 'Airwen' *(Eirwen)* has been telling you about . . . 'Airless'? *(Eirlys)* concerning Ingrid Bergman in a shop?

YOUNG MOS: No! Eirwen has been telling us about Gladys Aylward!

GREGG: Whoa! 'Airwen'; 'Airless' – and now Gladys? Who the hell is Gladys!

YOUNG MOS: Don't you know who Gladys Aylward is? I thought you said you worked with the film!

GREGG: I assist, sure!

YOUNG MOS: Then why don't you know who Gladys Aylward is!

FOR A SECOND, GREGG IS STUMPED.

GREGG: I'm waiting for you to tell me. You seem to know just about everything else!

YOUNG MOS: She was the missionary who went to China to save the children from the Japs!

GREGG: **That** Gladys! Hell, I know all about **her!** Would I be assisting Mark Robson, otherwise?

YOUNG MOS: 'Ai-weh-deh' the Chinese called her, Eirwen said. That means a very good person. I don't know what the Japanese called her . . .

GREGG: (HE CHUCKLES) Target practice!

YOUNG MOS: I'm writing an essay for Mr. Pritchard in the big school! It's all about the film . . . and Gladys Aylward . . . and the Chinese and Japs!

GREGG: Don't forget Ingrid.

YOUNG MOS: Oh, yes! She's the most important thing of all! Will she be a good Gladys you think?

GREGG: Who can tell! Will I . . . be a good me, ever?

YOUNG MOS: What?

GREGG: Listen, is there some place to stay around here?

YOUNG MOS: You should be at the Goat Hotel! Everybody's there . . .

GREGG: Well, I'm not! I'm here, talking to you!

YOUNG MOS: No point, anyway. It's full.

GREGG: Not anymore it ain't; there's a room going begging; I had an exchange of views with the management and was invited to leave.

YOUNG MOS: You could try the hostel! The youth hostel . . . two miles on.

GREGG: Swell. Look, I gotta go . . .

YOUNG MOS: My name is Moses Glyn Parry!

GREGG: I didn't ask.

YOUNG MOS: But everybody calls me 'Mos': my mother . . . father . . . and everybody! Even the head in the big school calls me Mos!

GREGG: Would that be the biblical 'Moses'?

YOUNG MOS: My father's middle name! And my grandfather, when he was alive. What's your name?

GREGG: What does your father do? What are you folks – farmers? What . . ?

YOUNG MOS HESITATES.

GREGG: What's this? Has the font of all knowledge run dry all of a sudden? Have I found the key to everlasting silence at last?

YOUNG MOS: He's a shepherd . . !

GREGG: Now that is biblical.

YOUNG MOS: Farmer, too! But he's not here! And I'm not going to be one . . . or the other.

GREGG: Be what you like.

YOUNG MOS: Not my father. Not me.

GREGG:	Your own man. Film star! The obvious choice around here.
YOUNG MOS:	Miss Jones said it first, not me. When we did Aladdin in the small school, she said I was the best Aladdin since . . . since nineteen twenty six or something!
GREGG:	And movies hadn't even been invented then!
YOUNG MOS:	No! What . . ?
GREGG:	They had silent movies, I guess, but they'd be no good to you. You'd have to be in the talkies!
YOUNG MOS:	'You making fun of me?
GREGG:	Dressed like that, I'd say you were a sitting duck. Gregg! My name is Gregg Grosvenor. 'You any the wiser? I'll be out of your life in two minutes; you'll probably never see me again!
YOUNG MOS:	Not if I come to see the filming of the film!
GREGG:	You won't see me, partner. I'm gonna be way too busy.
YOUNG MOS:	Assisting.
GREGG:	That's right! And anyway, you'll be busy yourself rounding up all them Indians!
YOUNG MOS:	Have you ever seen a proper Indian?
GREGG:	Has an Eskimo seen snow? (HE GRINS TO HIMSELF) I'll let you into a little secret: I'm a bit of an Indian myself as a matter of fact . . .

YOUNG MOS: *Argol!* (Goodness!) Are you? A Redskin! A real Redskin! *Argol hedd!* (Goodness me!)

GREGG: Sort of. Quarter say?

YOUNG MOS: Blackfoot; Crow; Apache . . . what?

GREGG: Hunkpapa: that's a small tribe of the Sioux confederacy.

YOUNG MOS: From where . . ?

GREGG: Why, the U. S. of A. of course!

YOUNG MOS: No – if you are quarter Indian, where did it come from – mother or father?

GREGG: Father; he was half Sioux. (HE PAUSES; AND FONDLY REMEMBERS) But my mother could be Indian too, some days . . .

YOUNG MOS: I don't understand.

GREGG: Or Mexican! Or . . . a tall, elegant ship sailing the yonder blue sea.

YOUNG MOS: She was a sailor?

GREGG: She was my mother, dummy! Don't you ever pretend, with yours?

YOUNG MOS: Not now! I'm nearly a man!

GREGG: (KINDLY) Sure you are.

YOUNG MOS: I am! And I'm old enough to know that you might not be telling me the whole truth . . !

GREGG: How come?

YOUNG MOS: Wel . . . for one thing, Grosvenor isn't an Indian name . . .

GREGG: Certainly not. I only use it on rare occasions.

YOUNG MOS: What is it, when you do use it?

GREGG: Red Tomahawk.

YOUNG MOS: *Argol!* (Goodness!)

HE POINTS HIS 'GUN' AT GREGG.

YOUNG MOS: 'The only good Injun is a dead Injun'.

HE 'SHOOTS'.

GREGG: 'Ever seen a dead Indian?

YOUNG MOS: It's what happens in the pictures.

GREGG: What . . . happens?

YOUNG MOS: It's what they say.

GREGG: What do they say?

PAUSE

GREGG: Do you know what they did to the Indians; what they really did?

YOUNG MOS: **They** killed General Custard too!

GREGG: Smartass. How would you like it . . . if I was to say . . . if I was to say 'the only good **Englishman** is a dead Englishman'!

YOUNG MOS: I wouldn't mind. I'm Welsh.

GREGG: Smartass.

YOUNG MOS: (CHANGING TACK) Look! Up there! Moel Druman Mountain! Bigger than all the rest! See? My father says . . . that a bird flies to the top, once every hundred years, and pecks at it with his beak, and a tiny little bit falls away. Then a different bird comes back in another hundred years and pecks off a little bit more. When the last bit falls, that will be the end of time . . .

GREGG: Farmer; shepherd; poet!

YOUNG MOS: I won't be here!

GREGG: You probably won't be here in fifty years, never mind the end of time!

YOUNG MOS: I read in the 'Weekly News' that a woman in Spain had lived to be a hundred and twenty!

GREGG: Kid, you're not woman! You're not Ingrid Bergman and you're not Spanish!

PAUSE

GREGG: Hell, I've got to find a bed for the night . . .

YOUNG MOS: On a clear day, you can see seventeen lakes!

GREGG: Excuse me . . ?

YOUNG MOS: From the top of Cnicht mountain!

GREGG: Is that German?

YOUNG MOS: In one go; from the top; looking down. My father . . . he's seen them all. I will too, one day.

GREGG: Yeah, sure, me too.

YOUNG MOS: No, impossible.

GREGG: What is?

YOUNG MOS: You and the mountain. You could never reach the top on your own!

GREGG: Oh no? Why's that? Is it . . . forbidden? Are these lakes . . . sacred or something? Or maybe the mountain is! Don't tell me! It's teeming with Indians . . ?

YOUNG MOS: It's . . . too far! You have to go along the Roman road first, and that's three miles long! Bwlch Batal then – for another two miles before you even start to climb!
(HE PAUSES) But I could take you if you like. If . . . !

GREGG: What?

YOUNG MOS: If you fix it for me to meet Ingrid Bergman!

GREGG: 'You crazy?

YOUNG MOS: You couldn't fix it? Is that because you're only an assistant . . ?

GREGG: Listen, I'm the chief! I'm Mr. Robson's **chief** assistant. Do you realise what that entails? Communicating on a daily basis – that's right, **daily** basis – between Mr. Robson and the Ingrid herself. I'm the bridge, boy – connecting star and star-maker. I'm an intimate, goddamit!

YOUNG MOS: Can you fix it?

FOR THE MOMENT, GREGG ENJOYS HIS NON-EXISTENT POWERS.

GREGG: Sure. I can fix anything. I can get you . . . anything.

YOUNG MOS: Have you got a camera! You could take my picture with Miss Bergman! Miss Bergman and me.

GREGG: O.K.! I fix it with Ingrid; you take me up the magical mountain. It's a deal.

YOUNG MOS: (GIVES THE ACCENT A 'GO') Sure thing, partner!

GREGG LAUGHS; SHAKES HIS HEAD IN SLIGHT DISBELIEF.

YOUNG MOS: Is it true what they say about her? I read it in the 'Weekly News'!

GREGG: Is what true?

YOUNG MOS: That she's living in sin. Where is that?

GREGG: Hey! Nobody, but nobody is that dumb! (HE PAUSES) It means Roberto Rossellini in her case I guess.

YOUNG MOS: Is that a country?

GREGG: You're having me on! (HE CONSIDERS) Maybe not.

A SINGLE BARREL OF A 12-BORE SHOTGUN GOES OFF, QUITE NEAR. GREGG IS STARTLED.

GREGG: As the mayor of Hiroshima once said: what the fuck was that!

YOUNG MOS LAUGHS, BUT WITHOUT KNOWING EXACTLY WHY PERHAPS.

GWYNETH PARRY COMES INTO VIEW. AT FIRST GLANCE SHE IS A STRANGE, ALMOST FRIGHTENING SIGHT, WITH HER MAN'S CAP, AND WEATHER-BEATEN, MAN'S RAINCOAT REACHING NEARLY TO THE GROUND, AND HER WELLINGTON BOOTS. THE DOUBLE-BARRELLED, 12-BORE SHOTGUN RESTING IN THE CRADLE OF HER ARM DOES NOT EXACTLY INSPIRE CONFIDENCE. SHE IS ABOUT THIRTY FIVE YEARS OF AGE: A GOOD-LOOKING WOMAN, OLD BEFORE HER TIME.

GREGG: What in God's name is that!

YOUNG MOS: That's my mother, shooting rabbits.

GREGG: [That's a man!]

GREGG: She's dressed like a man!

YOUNG MOS: All women dress like men around here!

GWYNETH: (SHE SEES THEM NOW) *Cer am y tŷ, Mos.* (Go to the house, Mos).

GREGG: (GIVING HER THE ONCE OVER) Did you say your papa was away?

GWYNETH: *Cer am y tŷ'r munud 'ma!* (Go to the house at once!)

YOUNG MOS EXITS.

GREGG: Hi there!

GWYNETH: Who are you; what do you want?

GREGG: I'm looking for a place to stay.

GWYNETH: Not here.

GREGG: Obviously not. No way am I gonna argue with that beauty! (THE GUN)

GWYNETH: I expect you're with this film nonsense . . ! This . . . 'sick' something!

GREGG: Is it that: nonsense?

GWYNETH: It's not honest sweat. Well, are you?

GREGG: [Maybe; maybe not.

GWYNETH: Talking like that? How silly of me, you must be local!

GREGG: Don't you have tourists in these parts?

GWYNETH: We have the English; the English are enough.

GREGG: Your boy seems to find them an endless source of amusement!

GWYNETH: He doesn't know anything.]

PAUSE.

GREGG: I'm the assistant director; [the chief . . . assistant. The bridge.

GWYNETH: Bridge?

GREGG: I bring good news – and bad.]

GWYNETH IS NATURALLY INTRIGUED, BUT WITHOUT WANTING TO GIVE TOO MUCH AWAY.

GWYNETH: [It's mostly bad around here.]

GREGG: [Then I can help you out . . .

GWYNETH: You don't say!]

GREGG: 'Buy some of your food stuff? I saw the sign . . .

GWYNETH: I thought you were looking for a place to stay . . ?

PAUSE.

GWYNETH: There's a cottage down the valley. Ask at the next big farm; ask for Mr. Gresham.

GREGG: What about eggs? Milk, too . . .

GWYNETH: (DOESN'T WANT TO APPEAR TOO KEEN) All sold out. Sorry!

GREGG: Uh . . . don't hens lay every day? And cows . . . whatever they do . . .

GWYNETH: I have my regular customers.

GREGG: (CHEERFULLY) O.K!

GREGG MAKES TO GO.

GWYNETH: Don't you have a name . . !

GREGG SMILES TO HIMSELF.

GWYNETH: (EXPLAINING) Different packets . . . for different people. Everybody in their place. You wouldn't want to end up with gooseberries, for sure.

GREGG: [So . . . shall I call by tomorrow?]

GWYNETH: [You do as you like! It's a free country . . .

GREGG: It is for you with that gun!

GWYNETH: 'Only a tool; as natural as life itself.]

HE IS QUITE CHARMED BY THAT.

GREGG: The name's Gregg; the name of the film is 'Inn of the Sixth Happiness'.

SHE HALF-SMILES – ALMOST. SHE TURNS TO GO. GREGG GETS A CAMERA OUT OF HIS RUCKSACK AND TAKES A PICTURE. THE RESPONSE FROM GWYNETH IS IMMEDIATE.

GWYNETH: What are you doing! Don't . . !

SHE ADJUSTS THE SHOTGUN UPWARDS.

GREGG: Whoa! Hold it!

GWYNETH: Don't do that! I don't like it!

GREGG: I was taking a picture for crying out loud . . !

GWYNETH: I don't belong to you!

GWYNETH TAKES A MENACING STEP FORWARD, ADJUSTING THE GUN SO THAT IT POINTS DIRECTLY AT GREGG.

GREGG: Easy! Just . . . back off, will you? Does your husband know you've got that thing!

FOR THE FIRST TIME, GWYNETH IS SEEN TO FALTER.

GWYNETH: (WITHOUT EMOTION) He isn't here at the moment.

THE LIGHT FADES. A NEW LIGHT COMES UP ON OLD MOS.

OLD MOS: *Take that cheap ring off . . . she said; people will talk*
It's not cheap! It cost a whole sixpence at Criciath Fair!
And father can't see me now!
Don't you believe in heaven? Take it off!
Take it off, and weep like everybody else.
'Can't weep: that will come when I'm least expecting it
Or not at all.
Let me go to Bwlch Batal, where the Romans are . . !
Where you're only dead until you count to twenty
Where every mother loves her son without condition
Before, and after batlle
Where Miss Wilias, Sunday-school teacher takes it from
behind without complaining.
(PAUSE)
Wait . . . she said. Don't rush. Life's too soon as it is.
Place it firm against your shoulder . . . just as he did,
every waking day, with left eye closed and feet slightly
apart, like a proper man.
Shoot, my boy! They're pests, not pets
Never let the horses smell the fear in you
Fear! Me! . . . who killed the half-breed on Clogwyn
Mawr with a single bullet?
Who rode with Custer and Cochise and lived to tell the
tale!
Who took the pipe with Sitting Bull on the eve of the
fateful rain dance; the night of the fatal dawn when he
was betrayed by his own, in Welsh fashion.
Don't tell me about death . . ! Show me the truth!
Is it true what they say about Jesus?
Is he hiding in the mountain? Or in Gerynt barn?
Has **he** got a gun?
Whistle down the wind with Hayley!
Open my eyes to the longed-for truth
Show me – before I look elsewhere.

THE LIGHT FADES ON OLD MOS. THE LIGHT COMES UP ON GREGG, WEARING RAY-BAN SUNGLASSES. HE'S SUFFERING A HANGOVER. HE RUMMAGES IN HIS RUCKSACK, GETS OUT AN ALMOST EMPTY HALF BOTTLE OF WHISKEY. HE CONSIDERS FINISHING IT OFF, BUT FINALLY DECIDES AGAINST IT, AND STUFFS THE BOTTLE BACK INSIDE THE RUCKSACK. YOUNG MOS APPEARS, AS BEFORE (COWBOY). HE IS CARRYING A BOTTLE OF WHITE, 'CORONA'-TYPE LEMONADE. HE FIRES HIS TOY GUN.

GREGG: Holy cow!

YOUNG MOS: Howdy, mister!

GREGG: Is your mom about . . ? Has she got any milk for me, do you know? Like now!

YOUNG MOS: Did you see Miss Bergman?

GREGG: [What . . ?

YOUNG MOS: Did you speak to her!]

GREGG: What's that you've got there?

YOUNG MOS: Did you speak to her?

GREGG: Is it soda? Gimme some, will you . . ?

YOUNG MOS: Why aren't you filming the film today?

GREGG: D'you mind . . ! . . . giving me some of that stuff?

YOUNG MOS: [Did you speak to her . . ?

GREGG: Yes!]

YOUNG MOS: Will she see me?

GREGG: Yes, she'll see you!

YOUNG MOS: When . . ?

GREGG: Soon! Gimme the fucking soda!

GREGG GRABS THE BOTTLE AND DRINKS DEEPLY.

YOUNG MOS: (DREAMILY) Soon . . .

GREGG: Boy, that's better . . !

HE DRINKS AGAIN, BEFORE HANDING THE BOTTLE BACK TO YOUNG MOS.

GREGG: I couldn't find the well! At the cottage . . . no running water. The guy said something about a well . . . but I couldn't find the damn thing in the dark! (HE PAUSES) Listen, I'm sorry about that word back there: it's a bad word, O.K.? I only use it on rare occasions, understand?

YOUNG MOS: Like Red Tomahawk . . ?

GREGG: What . . !

YOUNG MOS: Your Indian name!

GREGG: Oh! Sure, as rare as that.

YOUNG MOS: I don't mind.

GREGG: You won't hear it again; not from me.

YOUNG MOS: I don't mind . . . because I've heard my father say it a hundred times. 'Specially when Pero goes inside the sheep instead of around. I once heard him say it six times in the same sentence, with very little in between.

GREGG: Well . . ! If you're used to it . . ! You should've said! So . . . uh . . . where's your buddy, couldn't he make it? What's his name again?

YOUNG MOS: Alwyn Fedw!

GREGG: No, no . . . his cowboy name.

YOUNG MOS: Pretty!

GREGG: You're Charlie, right . . ?

YOUNG MOS: He's collecting cows with his father . . .

GREGG: Really? 'Sounds great.

YOUNG MOS: [You can be Pretty if you like . . !

GREGG: Uh . . . no. No, I'm not equipped. No gun, no horse. I'd be a liability.

YOUNG MOS: You can borrow one of mine!

GREGG: You have two horses?

YOUNG MOS: Two guns!

HE OFFERS GREGG HIS WOODEN TOY GUN.

GREGG: No. Look, it's early. I'll pass.

YOUNG MOS: What about Hokka . . ! We could play him.

GREGG: Who . . ?

YOUNG MOS: Hokka! Bandit leader! Friend of Miss Bergman. I mean . . . Gladys Aylward!]

GREGG: [Uh-huh.

YOUNG MOS: When the Japs attacked . . . the Chinese didn't know what to do with the prisoners. The Mandarin wanted to chop their heads off . . . before the Japs could do it – if you know what I mean. But Ingrid Bergman said no and saved the day!

GREGG: It's a movie, O.K.?]

A PAUSE.

YOUNG MOS: Did you speak to Miss Bergman? Did you tell her about me . . !

GREGG: Do you have a short memory?

YOUNG MOS: 'Soon' you said. When will that be?

GREGG: When the great Ingrid gives me the nod! But she won't be rushed. And she might change her mind any second! Be warned! Y'see, she's a very private individual; sitting there between takes, minding her own business.

YOUNG MOS: What's 'takes'?

GREGG: It's a technical term, don't worry about it. She sits in her folding chair, a little distance from the crowd, the legs of her Chinese pants rolled up, maybe looking at her script. Then, my friend Mark Robson comes along; and Miss Bergman, she's sitting there, and Mark comes up and whispers gently: 'Ready now, Ingrid', and off she goes obediently, back to the lights and cameras. Me? I'd tell her: 'Bergman, get your asshole over here now!'

YOUNG MOS: *Argol!* (Goodness!) Really? But . . . she's a film star!

GREGG: She still has to visit the john, my friend! Don't get too excited. It's all . . . transitory. In a few weeks it'll be over and done with. (HE PAUSES TO REFLECT) There for you one minute, all warm and comforting – the next, gone. Keep your distance.

YOUNG MOS: But I don't want to . . !

GREGG: Fuck; why bother?

YOUNG MOS: You've used that word again!

GREGG: (HE GRINS) Yup!

A PAUSE.

YOUNG MOS: Do you think . . . I could get some work with the film? You could fix it for me! They're looking for children all the time, Now Beudy Glas was telling me! Buying them, for two pounds a day . . .

GREGG: I think you'll find they're paying folks for their services.

YOUNG MOS: That's . . . ! . . . ten pounds for working five days! (HE PAUSES) My father . . .

GREGG: I meant to ask you about him.

YOUNG MOS: (HESITATES A LITTLE) He has to work seven days, in all weather, for half of that.

GREGG: Does he work away?

YOUNG MOS: (EMPHATICALLY) Yes! Away! For a long time!

GREGG: Not that I'm sticking my nose in or anything, but . . ! Your mother said . . . what's her name by the way?

YOUNG MOS: Gwyneth.

GREGG: (SAVOURING IT) Gwyn . . . eth. That's a beautiful name. My mother's name . . . is Edith.

YOUNG MOS: That's horrible!

GREGG: (COMES ON STRONG) Son, you're a careless word away from death.

YOUNG MOS: No! I had an *Anti* (Auntie) Edith once, and she was really horrible. She had a *mwstash* (moustache) and looked like a walrus. Honest!

GREGG: And every other Edith is nice?

YOUNG MOS: Yes! Perfect.

GREGG: I like that. (HE PAUSES) So . . . what about your father?

YOUNG MOS: 'Told you; he's away.

GREGG: I meant his name.

YOUNG MOS: Is it important?

GREGG WAITS FOR AN ANSWER.

YOUNG MOS: Alun.

GREGG: Say again . . ?

YOUNG MOS: Alun! (HE PAUSES) Have you got a father?

GREGG: 'Here, aint I?

YOUNG MOS: What does he do? Is he with the films . . !

GREGG: Hell no! (HE CONSIDERS QUITE HARD BEFORE TELLING HIM) I've no idea. He walked out on us when I was a kid.

YOUNG MOS: Where did he walk to?

GREGG: He vanished. Never to return.

YOUNG MOS: (INTERNAL) Never to return.

GREGG: Y'see, you're lucky: your father's coming back.

YOUNG MOS: What about your mother?

GREGG STARES AT HIM, UNTIL HE BECOMES UNCOMFORTABLE.

YOUNG MOS: (HELPFULLY) Maybe it was the Indian in him!

GREGG: The what . . !

YOUNG MOS: Your father! Looking for fresh hunting ground! (HE FALTERS A BIT) Looking for . . . buffalo.

GREGG: Of course! I never thought of that.

YOUNG MOS: It's what they do! They wander . . . from place to place.

PAUSE

YOUNG MOS: Do you call your father 'syr' (sir), like in the films?

PAUSE

YOUNG MOS: How old are you . . !

GREGG: Am I older than your father, is that what you're asking? Does it matter?

YOUNG MOS: You'll always be older.

GREGG: (AFTER SOME CONSIDERATION): So . . . where is he?

YOUNG MOS: Standing on the mountain in green pyjamas, listening to the thin wind and smiling.

GREGG: What . . !

GWYNETH APPEARS, SAME AS BEFORE, MINUS THE SHOTGUN.

GWYNETH: *Ma' dy fwyd ti ar y bwr' yn oeri! Dos!* (Your food is getting cold! Go!)

YOUNG MOS EXITS.

GREGG: Is he in trouble? Blame me! 'Kept him talking, I'm afraid. Or maybe it was the other way round. He's quite a guy! How are you today?

GWYNETH HAS A SMALL PACKAGE. SHE OFFERS IT TO GREGG.

GWYNETH: Half a dozen eggs and a pint of milk.

GREGG: That's terrific!

HE TAKES THE PACKAGE AND GRINS.

GREGG: That's my name! Right there!

GWYNETH: How did you find Mr. Gresham?

GREGG: I looked under a rock, and there he was!

GWYNETH: (PO-FACED) Yes, very good. Very funny.

GREGG: He's kinda . . . weird, ain't he?

GWYNETH: Did he give you the cottage?

GREGG: He gave me a drink! And then another! And another . . .

GWYNETH: Yes, I can smell it from here.

GREGG: Must've given me the once-over, ten times or more, if you get my meaning . . .

GWYNETH: He is . . . different. He doesn't speak the spoke.

GREGG: What . . ?

GWYNETH: . . . my language.

GREGG: Uh . . . no; that's not what I meant.

GWYNETH: He's from another place.

GREGG: Just like me!

GWYNETH: Not like you. He's here to stay.

GREGG: And I'm not? What do I detect – regret, or satisfaction?

BUT GWYNETH DOES NOT BETRAY ANY PARTICULAR EMOTION.

GREGG: Say . . ! How much do I owe you for these? I don't have a cent on me right now!

GWYNETH: Pay me again.

GREGG: You trust me . . ?

GWYNETH: (SIMPLY) I have no choice.

GREGG: Doesn't he give you enough?

GWYNETH: Sorry . . ?

GREGG: Let's see if I can remember this . . ! Ailyn . . ? (ALUN) Am I close?

GWYNETH: I don't know what you're talking about.

GREGG: You get to keep all of the egg money, right?

GWYNETH: It's not much, I tell you straight. Egg money won't kill me, and that's certain!

GREGG: D'you know what you should do . . ! And maybe – just maybe – I could help you here. Uh . . . did I tell you I was assistant director on the 'Sixth Happiness' . . ?

GWYNETH: You couldn't help me.

GREGG: Now that's where you're wrong! If you . . . played your cards right, I could get you an introduction!

GWYNETH: Introduction . . ?

GREGG: I could have a word with the location manager on your behalf; they're always looking for extra transport on the shoot. You must have transport of sorts.

GWYNETH: No thank you. I want to be told what to do by the sun, the moon and the seasons, not by strangers who are here today and gone tomorrow . . .

GREGG: I believe they're paying five English pounds a day . . .

41

GWYNETH: I do know.

GREGG: Of course, you'd have to supply your own gas.

GWYNETH: I said 'no thank you'!

GREGG: Receiving you loud and clear.

GWYNETH: And that goes for Mos as well!

GREGG: That's a shame. 'Told me he wanted to be a film star someday!

GWYNETH: Film star indeed!

GREGG: Just like John Wayne! He was a farmer's boy, once!

GWYNETH: No good to me. He might as well wish for wings, and fly to the top of Llechwedd Ganol and back!

GREGG: He's sweet on Ingrid Bergman, that's his problem!

GWYNETH SNORTS HER DISAPPROVAL. HER REACTION DOES NOT SURPRISE GREGG. HE DECIDES TO 'PLAY' ON THIS.

GREGG: I've tried to make him see the error of his ways!

GWYNETH: A married woman – a mother! – carrying on with another man! Having that man's children! It's not our way, around here. Not when you're sworn to another man!

GREGG: It doesn't always work out that way!

GWYNETH: I wouldn't have the front to go out the back door! Animals have better manners!

GREGG: Excuse me . . ?

GWYNETH: She's a loose mother, and that's all there is to it.

GREGG: Come on, that's rather strong, ain't it? Nobody's that bad. She's a mother . . !

GWYNETH: And it's the children who always suffer! I mean to say, does the 'Weekly News' give tuppence about the state of little Isabella and Ingrid Junior, locked away in that strange village?

GREGG: It's not strange! It's a charming Italian folly! I'm sure Roberto is very much at home!

GWYNETH: (GIVING IN) I don't know the woman.

GREGG: Well, you wouldn't.

GWYNETH: Only by her sight. She might be very nice. I've only ever seen her in the pictures.

GREGG: Casablanca?

GWYNETH: (REMEMBERING) Yes. Yes, a long time back. I remember. Good story.

GREGG: Love . . . story.

GWYNETH: I remember.

GREGG: (SUGGESTIVELY) The film . . . or other activities? 'Just thinking aloud!

GWYNETH: What do you mean?

GREGG: You're Gwyneth, right? Can I call you that, or would you prefer Mrs. Parry? (A BEAT) Tell me, Gwyneth . . . ! . . . don't you get lonely when he's away? Young Mos was telling me that he's away quite a lot.

GWYNETH: Don't listen to Mos. He's living in dreams.

GREGG: Celluloid dreams?

GWYNETH: *Seliw* what? Is that rude?

GREGG: 'Of all the gin joints in all the towns in all the world, she walks into mine'.

GWYNETH: (REMEMBERING; IN HER OWN, UNSEXY ACCENT) *Play it for me, Sam.*

GREGG: Very romantic!

GWYNETH NAILS HIM WITH A LOOK.

GREGG: So . . . what d'you get up to? Is it a case of 'whilst shepherds watch their flock at night' it's party time back at the homestead?

GWYNETH: That's a forward thing to say to a stranger.

GREGG: Don't worry, I'm only fooling! 'Didn't mean to offend. 'Wouldn't want to mess with a mountain man, no siree!

GWYNETH: You have nothing to worry about. Alun won't hurt you now.

THE LIGHT FADES ON GREGG AND GWYNETH. A LIGHT COMES UP ON OLD MOS.

OLD MOS: *Ifan . . .* she once said, *drove me to the hospital in his cold van that day*

I had to work the broken wiper with my right hand
His left hand resting on my knee
Life goes on, I suppose.
Hurt. Death. Grief.
The long wailing from the room next door; from her half-empty bed, like Black Rock Sands with the tide out in its extreme
Life goes on.
There's sheep-shearing day to come:
Twelve hungry men and a silent kitchen?
Then no more:
It was the Yanks coming to the rescue across the tear-stained expanse
Life goes on, I suppose.

THE LIGHT FADES. THE LIGHT COMES UP. YOUNG MOS APPEARS IN HIS COWBOY GEAR, RIDING AN IMAGINARY HORSE.

YOUNG MOS: Whoa, boy! Hold it, men! O.K., we camp here! Jake, take care of the horses!

HE 'DISMOUNTS'; CHECKS THE LAY OF THE LAND.

YOUNG MOS: Will, make a fire and put the beans on!

GREGG APPEARS, UNBEKNOWN TO YOUNG MOS. HE HAS HIS RUCKSACK SLUNG OVER HIS SHOULDER.

YOUNG MOS: You take first watch, Elmer! What's that you say, Pretty?

GREGG: Indians, Charlie, out on the far ridge!

YOUNG MOS: *Blydi hel!* (Bloody hell!) How long have you been there . . !

GREGG: (IN 'CHARACTER') I'm stranded! 'Had to shoot my horse!

YOUNG MOS: (HIMSELF) With what?

GREGG: Two fingers and bang?

HE MAKES THE SHAPE OF A GUN WITH HIS HAND.

YOUNG MOS: Do you want to use this? (HIS TOY GUN) You can be Pretty if you like!

GREGG: I'll sit this one out.

YOUNG MOS: Did you see Ingrid Bergman? Is it alright?

GREGG: I'm making progress on that front!

YOUNG MOS: Did she say 'yes'?

GREGG: Signs are good.

YOUNG MOS: When!

GREGG: (DELIBERATELY CHANGING TACK) Look – gimme the gun.

YOUNG MOS: You want to play?

GREGG: (IN 'CHARACTER') Charlie, just gimme that darn gun!

YOUNG MOS: Let's play 'goodies' and 'baddies' . . .

GREGG: Whatever you say, partner!

YOUNG MOS: I'm the 'goodie'! And . . . you're the 'baddie'. We're in the mountain, shooting at each other! I kill you.

GREGG: Not if I kill you first!

YOUNG MOS: You haven't got a gun.

YOUNG MOS GRINS, AND THROWS OVER HIS TOY GUN.

YOUNG MOS: Look out! It's loaded.

YOUNG MOS PULLS THE WOODEN HANDGUN FROM HIS BELT.

YOUNG MOS: Ready?

GREGG: Sure, I'm ready.

WITHOUT WARNING, GREGG FIRES HIS GUN (TINNY BANG).

GREGG: 'See? 'Said I'd get you first!

YOUNG MOS: Missed! (HE AIMS HIS WOODEN GUN) Bang! Bang!

GREGG: (DUCKING) What a lousy shot!

GREGG SHOOTS.

YOUNG MOS: Missed again!

BOTH TAKE COVER. IN THE ENSUING 'BATTLE', YOUNG MOS FIRES FOUR MORE TIMES, GREGG THRICE. GRINNING, GREGG BREAKS COVER, COMES OUT INTO THE OPEN.

YOUNG MOS: Bang! Bang! Bang! You're dead!

GREGG: No, no. I'm not dead. You're dead.

GREGG SHOOTS.

GREGG: I've got bullets left. You're spent.

YOUNG MOS: I'm not! Bang! Bang!

GREGG: Yes, you are! You fired your last, five bullets ago! I counted.

YOUNG MOS: No, I didn't! Alright, yes I did, but it doesn't matter because I re-loaded!

GREGG: When, for crying out loud!

YOUNG MOS: When you turned away!

GREGG: Come on! I could not have been turned away for more than two seconds! 'Impossible to re-load in that time! It takes twelve and a half seconds to re-load a Colt-45, or a gun of similar stature . . . even if the target is passive . . . which I certainly was not! I'm trying . . . to tell you about the rules, Mos. There are . . . rules, which must be obeyed.

YOUNG MOS: Stupid rules! My father let me win every time!

GREGG: (HE PAUSES) Your father. So, what's the story there? What happened . . . exactly? (HE PAUSES) Is . . . your mother over it now?

YOUNG MOS: He fell on the mountain.

GREGG: And you want to take me up there . . !

YOUNG MOS: Not before I see Ingrid Bergman. That was the deal.

GREGG: I told you: the signs are good.

A PAUSE.

YOUNG MOS: He isn't dead. Not really.

GREGG: No . . ?

YOUNG MOS: He's standing on the top in green pyjamas, listening to the thin wind and smiling.

GREGG: Right. Maybe . . . he's looking for those seventeen lakes of yours?

YOUNG MOS: Not looking now. He's there. But . . . he wasn't, in the beginning. He was lying down in a dark room . . .

GREGG: (REMEMBERING) . . . in a dark box, in a dark room. And then she got up and walked away, leaving only tears behind.

MOS: 'She' . . ?

GREGG: The dead! Don't they get all the luck?

YOUNG MOS: I don't understand.

GREGG: There should be a warning about it.

YOUNG MOS: Is 'she . . '?

GREGG: (CHANGING TACK) Tell me about the lakes!

YOUNG MOS: I know them all by name! The lakes . . .

GREGG: All seventeen? Who taught you? Your mother, I bet! Tell me about her, Mos . . .

YOUNG MOS: Llyn Gwynant! Llyn Dinas – they're easy, my dad said. Big and easy through the mist. Llyn Llagi; Llyn Biswail; Llyn Edno . . .

GREGG: What's "llyn"? (PRONOUNCED 'CLIN')

YOUNG MOS: Lake! Of course. . . Cerrig y Myllt, large and small; Foel; Llydaw; Clogwyn Brith; Llyn Coch . . .

GREGG: Teach me! Teach me how to say the words! 'To speak . . . the spoke . . .'

YOUNG MOS: All of them?

GREGG: 'You crazy? No, one or two. Just gimme enough ammo to impress.

YOUNG MOS: What about . . . Llyn Dinas . . . ?

GREGG: Llyn . . . ('CLIN' AGAIN) Dinas . . . yeah, 'got that.

YOUNG MOS: And Llyn Coch . . .

GREGG: That's a good 'un. Llyn . . ?

YOUNG MOS: Coch!

GREGG: Coch! ('COCK')

YOUNG MOS GIGGLES.

GREGG: Wassa matter!

YOUNG MOS: Nothing!

GREGG: Right. Llyn Dinas; Llyn Coch; Llyn Dinas . . . Llyn Coch. (HIS PRONUNCIATION IS ALL OVER THE PLACE).

YOUNG MOS IDLY OBSERVES GREGG'S RUCKSACK, ON THE DECK. OUT OF ITS SEMI-OPEN TOP PROTRUDES THE PORN MAGAZINE, PREVIOUSLY SEEN. YOUNG MOS TAKES IT.

YOUNG MOS: [Can I have a look . . ?

GREGG: What . . ?]

YOUNG MOS: *Blydi hel!* (BLOODY HELL) Naked women! And men . . ! What are they doing to each other?

GREGG: Hey, no, gimme that . . . Gimme it back before I really get mad!

YOUNG MOS RUNS OFF LAUGHING, CLUTCHING THE MAGAZINE.

GREGG: Fuck!

THE LIGHT GOES DOWN. A NEW LIGHT COMES UP ON OLD MOS.

OLD MOS: From smoking blotters to fine Virginia in one furious night
From longing to doing
From imagining to seeing
Beneath the hot quilt; hot and sticky, praying that my trusty Ever-Ready would last the course
All hands on deck
One short of cover to cover
I'm sorry, Pearl of Indonesia, for falling asleep before the liquid of your love could engulf me
No looking back from that night on
Even Miss Wilias, Sunday schoolteacher, forgotten, banished from my dreams to everlasting spinsterhood; the five planned children – at least! – eliminated, long before they could witness the beauty of trees, or appreciate the joy of swimming in a river in your birthday suit
No more black snow, and cold, unforgiving stones; a million stones, as far as my watery eyes could see
No more chores to kill the soul; no more death on the mountain
Hail my saviour from across the Atlantic, come to send me on my merry way towards the naked, waiting world – cock in hand.

THE LIGHT FADES ON OLD MOS. A NEW LIGHT COMES UP ON GWYNETH. A SHEPHERD'S CROOK HAS REPLACED THE GUN. SHE IS SEARCHING. GREGG APPEARS.

GREGG: Looking for anyone in particular?

GWYNETH: Fox.

GREGG: 'You aiming to catch him with that! (THE SHEPHERD'S CROOK) Where's the gun?

GWYNETH: Marking. His time will come.

GREGG: Am I . . . 'marked' Gwyneth?

GWYNETH: Should you be?

GREGG: I should be given a telling-off for what I said to you yesterday, for sure! I'm sorry about that. But I honestly didn't know at the time.

GWYNETH: Is that an excuse? Alive or dead, it shouldn't make any difference. I'm a married woman. No, a widow now. I deserve respect, not to be made a sport of!

GREGG: Hit me with that big stick.

GWYNETH: It's not a stick; it's not for play; it's for catching sheep.

GREGG: Is it . . . Alun's? (PRONOUNCED 'AILYN').

GWYNETH: Alun; his name was Alun. (PAUSE) He . . . was catching sheep, when . . . (BEAT) Rescuing, I should say.

GREGG: He fell, right? Mos was telling me . . !

GWYNETH: He shouldn't have said anything.

GREGG: Maybe he needs to talk . . ?

GWYNETH: Nonsense. It's over and done with. We have to get on with things. It's not our place to question.

GREGG: Ain't it? I do!

GWYNETH: You're American.

GREGG: God, all that stuff?

GWYNETH: It's not 'stuff'!

GREGG: Lady, I know what God does . . .

GWYNETH: Don't call me that!

GREGG: Sorry! It's just my American way. God takes your breath away.

GWYNETH: (AFTER A BEAT) Yes.

PAUSE.

GREGG: Where did he fall?

GWYNETH: Clogwyn Mawr. That's a big cliff. It wouldn't mean anything to you.

GREGG: (OPPORTUNISTICALLY) Would that be anywhere near Clin Cock? (LLYN COCH).

GWYNETH LOOKS PERPLEXED.

GREGG: Clin Cock! Don't you know your lakes?

53

GWYNETH: You do?

GREGG: Sure thing! That's why I'm here in a sense. I'm looking for my roots.

GWYNETH: You're American; don't be ridiculous.

GREGG: Not always! John Wayne wasn't always a movie star, remember? You see, Gwyneth, I have a hunch I might be half-Welsh, on my father's side.

GWYNETH: Really?

GREGG: As God's my witness . . !

GWYNETH: O! 'Believe in him now, do we?

GREGG: My father . . . he would say 'English', of course – but what did he know! O.K. – so did I before I came here. I have to be honest: I'd never heard of the Welsh until I landed in these parts . . .

GWYNETH: *Argol!* (Goodness!) No?

GREGG: But then . . . I don't suppose you've ever heard of the Hunkpapa people?

GWYNETH: You've got me there.

GREGG: Didn't Mos tell you? I'm quarter Hunkpapa: that's a small, but significant tribe of the Sioux confederacy? Sitting Bull's tribe. You must've heard of him!

GWYNETH: I've seen him in the pictures once or twice.

GREGG: Now we're getting somewhere!

GWYNETH: But . . . Sitting Bull wasn't Welsh!

GREGG: Not on the face of it. But he was at one with nature. And that's how I feel. Being here, in these mountains, the lakes . . .

GWYNETH: Have you actually seen all the lakes? It's not easy!

GREGG: (SOLEMNLY) I come all this way and not see the lakes?

IN TRUTH, GWYNETH'S A LITTLE IMPRESSED WITH THIS.

GWYNETH: That's . . . very interesting.

GREGG: 'Tell you what: get down the cottage one evening and I'll fill you in.

GWYNETH: Good grief, are you mad!

GREGG: We could have dinner or something. Nothing fancy – some spaghetti and wine, say . . .

GWYNETH: What do you take me for!

GREGG: Under all that protection? (THE CAP, ETC) Hard to tell! Look, we could talk about the film; discuss work maybe. Have you given it any more thought?

GWYNETH: I've told you once, I'll have nothing to do with it!

GREGG: Couldn't you use some extra in your pocket?

GWYNETH: And come to the cottage in return? I wasn't born yesterday!

GREGG: No! No, you've got it all wrong. I'm thinking . . . of your wellbeing. Mos's too.

GWYNETH: Why should you?

GREGG: Gwyneth, be proud by all means. But don't cut off your nose to spite your face.

PAUSE.

GREGG: (FEELS HE CAN PUSH IT ALONG) We won't talk about the film, if you'd rather not. There are . . . other things.

GWYNETH: Yes.

GREGG: Your choice!

THERE'S A 'LOOK' OF SORTS BETWEEN THEM.

GWYNETH: What is 'spaghetti'?

GREGG: You'll come? That's great!

GWYNETH: No, I'm asking what it is.

GREGG: Well . . ! It's kinda . . . y'know . . . it's kinda long . . . and thin . . ! . . . and you twist it around your fork and . . .

GWYNETH: *Argol!* (Goodness!) What kind of food is that?

GREGG: Come down the cottage and you'll find out.

GWYNETH: Food like that, it might do me harm!

SO SHE HASN'T SAID 'NO' THIS TIME. GREGG DECIDES TO TAKE A CALCULATED RISK.

GREGG: Can I ask you something?

GWYNETH: (LIGHTLY) I hope you're not going to ask me to cook it . . !

GREGG: Were you ever unfaithful?

GWYNETH: What . . . did you say?

GREGG: Have you ever made it with another guy? You know, since Ailyn (Alun) . . .

GWYNETH: What . . !!

GREGG: Or during the time you were lovers, I don't know! It happens!

WITHOUT WARNING, GWYNETH HITS HIM; SHE FLOORS HIM IN FACT, WITH A WELL-PLACED PUNCH, DRAWING A SMALL AMOUNT OF BLOOD. IT IS A NASTY SURPRISE FOR GREGG.

GREGG: Wow! O.K. let's talk spaghetti . . !

GWYNETH: I'm sorry . . !

GREGG: No, don't come near me!

GWYNETH: Don't be silly! You're hurt . . .

SHE EXAMINES THE DAMAGE.

GWYNETH: Look what you've gone and done!

SHE GETS A DIRTY HANKY AND DABS AT THE DAMAGED AREA A BIT.

GREGG: It happens, that's all I'm saying.

GWYNETH: Be quiet.

SHE CARRIES ON. GRADUALLY, A 'MOMENT' DEVELOPS BETWEEN THEM – BEFORE THEY BOTH BREAK AWAY ABRUPTLY. THEN A BRIEF AWKWARDNESS, BEFORE GWYNETH HANDS HIM THE DIRTY HANKY AND LEAVES. GREGG LOOKS AT HER GO, ALMOST LONGINGLY.

THE LIGHT FADES.

THE LIGHT COMES UP. GWYNETH AND YOUNG MOS APPEAR, THE FORMER BRANDISHING GREGG'S PORNOGRAPHIC MAGAZINE.

GWYNETH: *Lle cest ti'o! Lle cest ti'o, Mos!* (Where did you get it! Where did you get it, Mos!)

YOUNG MOS: *Dwad o hyd iddo fo wnes i!* (I found it!)

GWYNETH: *Clwydda! Y **fo** roth o i chdi!* (Lies! **He** gave it to you!)

YOUNG MOS: *Naci! Ffendio fo ar y mynydd wnes i!* (No! I found it on the mountain!)

GWYNETH: *Mi fydd hi'n waeth a'n't ti os na ddeudi di'r gwir!* (It'll be worse if you don't tell me the truth!)

YOUNG MOS: *'Dw'i yn deud y gwir!* (I am telling the truth!)

GWYNETH ROLLS UP THE MAGAZINE AND GRABS HOLD OF YOUNG MOS AND GIVES HIM A GOOD BEATING. NO HALF-MEASURES HERE, AND YOUNG MOS HOWLS. GREGG APPEARS.

GREGG: Hey . . . stop that! What's going on?

GWYNETH: This . . . is what's going on! (SHE THRUSTS THE MAGAZINE IN HIS FACE) This . . . filth!!

GREGG: Listen . . . I can explain!

GWYNETH: What is there to explain! You should be locked up, and when I see Bob Wilias, policeman, I'll tell him too!

GREGG: It's not what you think!

YOUNG MOS: *Nid y fo rhoth o i mi!* He didn't give it to me! (HE SAYS **BOTH** VERSIONS, IN THE TWO LANGUAGES)

GWYNETH: *Bistaw! A glua'i am y tŷ 'na cyn i mi hannar dy ladd di!* (That's enough! Off you go to the house before I skin you alive!)

SHE GIVES HIM A FINAL BELT WITH THE MAGAZINE.

YOUNG MOS: (TO GREGG) Sorry . . !

GWYNETH: *Mi fyddi di!* (You will be!)

YOUNG MOS RETREATS.

GREGG: Gwyneth, please . . .

GWYNETH: What are you? One of those funny people we hear so much about?

GREGG: Gwyneth, that's crazy . . .

GWYNETH: 'Mrs. Parry' to you! No, don't call me anything! And don't ever come near this place again!

GWYNETH STRIDES OFF.

GREGG BECOME AWARE OF THE SOUND OF TWO, SINGLE-ENGINED AIRCRAFTS APPROACHING. THE SOUND INCREASES BEFORE SETTLING INTO A CIRCULAR PATTERN, INCREASING AND DECREASING INTERMITTENTLY FROM THEN ON, DURING WHICH EXPLOSIVES GO OFF IN THE DISTANCE.

GREGG IS PERPLEXED AS THE LIGHT FADES.

A NEW LIGHT COMES UP ON OLD MOS.

OLD MOS: Sex hurts; it's written in the Bible: 'he who abuses himself, and stains the great-grandmother's handed-down quilt with unmentionables, will be caught and beaten with dead father's belt'.
Not only beaten bodily, but beaten in the race for love Losing Miss Wilias, Sunday schoolteacher from my dreams, to Llew the carpenter who thrust her into real life, and must have had her measured while my back was turned, was a particularly savage blow
And all of this pushing me into greater ignorance
(HE HALF-SMILES AS HE REMEMBERS):
When it happens, believe me, 'It's no joke what men and women do to each other'
For all my intimate knowledge of women's bodies in flash light, I still lacked the fundamentals:
Where do babies come from?
Do they come with Santa, down the chimney?
Is it once a year?
Who makes them?
Why do they die?
Do they get squashed in the narrow bend, or suffocate in his flowing beard?
If they die in the bringing, does he leave the milk and mince pies as a token of regret?
Can I be a rabbit, and pretend death doesn't exist?

THE LIGHT FADES ON OLD MOS. THE LIGHT COMES UP ON GREGG. HE IS ASLEEP, A NEARLY EMPTY, HALF-WHISKEY BOTTLE IN HIS HAND. YOUNG MOS APPEARS. GREGG SLOWLY COMES AROUND. HE HAS A MARK ON HIS FACE WHERE GWYNETH HIT HIM. HE IS QUITE PENSIVE.

YOUNG MOS: It was ours, once.

GREGG: Excuse me?

YOUNG MOS: This place: it was my father's land; his cottage; and his father before him.

GREGG: Moses and Son?

YOUNG MOS: He had to sell, after the big winter of 'forty seven. The sheep, they were all lost. Cattle too. But I don't remember . . .

PAUSE.

YOUNG MOS: What happened to you?

GREGG: 'Got drunk. 'Thrown out of the hotel bar.

MOS: I heard there was fighting! Chairs and bottles flying, just like 'Shane'!

GREGG: Only it wasn't. This was for real. (HE INDICATES THE MARK ON HIS FACE)

MOS: Celebrating . . ?

GREGG: Celebrating what! 'You kidding?

MOS: Bombing Yangcheng!

GREGG: Oh . . . sure. One hell of a party!

YOUNG MOS: I was on my way to watch . . ! To the top of Llechwedd Ganol. Everybody was going! Alwyn; Dora; Owi Bach; Lisi – everybody!
But I didn't get to see anything in the end.

GREGG: How come?

MOS SHIFTS AWKWARDLY.

GREGG: Caught red-handed, huh?

YOUNG MOS: She was in my room, cleaning. I was having tea, but not bread and jam as usual, no. (PROUDLY) I was having *sbigati* or something! Long, thin things in a can, with red sauce all over!

GREGG: Really? (THAT PLEASES HIM) 'She give you hell?

MOS: Worse than when she caught the gypsy boy stealing apples.

GREGG: Don't worry about it: I had a shit day too. Women, eh . . . (BITTERLY, IN A COD SWEDISH ACCENT) 'Go and get the coffee, boy!' I'm a grown man! (JOHN WAYNE NOW) 'The fuck I will! Go get it yourself, you Swedish whore!'

MOS: If you're talking about Miss Bergman, I don't like it.

GREGG: You don't have to live with it, pal! (A BEAT) She's playing . . . what . . . an English missionary? In a fucking stupid Swedish accent! In the same fucking stupid Swedish accent that she's used to play every goddam part in her entire fucking life! Hey, where's the truth in that! (SOFTLY NOW) 'Go get the coffee for your

	mamma. Come here. Gimme a kiss. Now go get the coffee'. 'See how easy it is?
MOS:	At least she didn't hit you.
GREGG:	You shouldn't have taken the magazine, buddy.
YOUNG MOS:	Why not! I'm old enough . . .
GREGG:	For what? You're talking through your ass.
YOUNG MOS:	'Lot of 'ass' in that magazine!
GREGG:	Jesus!

YOUNG MOS GRINS CHEEKILY.

GREGG:	Seriously: that magazine . . . y'know . . . it's not for someone of your age.
YOUNG MOS:	I'm nearly fourteen! And I've helped hundreds of sheep come with lamb! 'Specially when I was very young.
GREGG:	Does youth make you better qualified?
YOUNG MOS:	Small hands.
GREGG:	So . . . why ask what the man and woman were doing to each other?
YOUNG MOS:	Having a joke.
GREGG:	It's no joke what men and women do to each other.
YOUNG MOS:	I know all about it.
GREGG:	You'd run a mile if you came face to face with the real thing.

PAUSE

GREGG: How's your mother? 'She mad with me?

YOUNG MOS: Yes.

GREGG: Are you?

YOUNG MOS: (AWKWARDLY) I like you.

GREGG: Good! Good . . . (BEAT) 'Tell you what we'll do . . ! Let's go up that magical mountain of yours; 'maybe look for the seventeen lakes?

YOUNG MOS: Not before I meet Ingrid Bergman.

GREGG: Jesus Christ! (CHILDLIKE) Not before I meet Ingrid Bergman! Is that the only song you know? And hasn't it ever crossed your mind that **she** might not want to see **you?** She yearns to be in Mr. Rosellini's arms, my friend, not talking bull with some dreamer!

YOUNG MOS: I'm not a dreamer!

GREGG: Yes you damn well are! I got that from your own mother!

YOUNG MOS: You promised.

GREGG: Sure, I promised . . .

YOUNG MOS: Anybody would think you don't work with the film at all!

GREGG: Oh, they would, would they! Well, it's not possible. Let's . . . let's just call the whole deal off! No more promises, O.K.?

YOUNG MOS: That means you can change anything. Nothing is true.

GREGG: Well, forgive me for being the bearer of bad tidings here, but I think you'll find that that's the way it goes once you're out in the big, bad world!

YOUNG MOS: Then I'll stay where I am, thank you very much!

GREGG: Don't be a jerk! How the hell do you expect to become a hotshot film star, cocooned in this God-forsaken place?

YOUNG MOS: Meeting Ingrid Bergman would be a start.

GREGG GIVES MOS A LONG, LONG LOOK.

GREGG: O.K. friend, lemme come clean: I'm not . . . the assistant director on this movie.

MOS STARES AT HIM IN DISBELIEF.

GREGG: I'm not! I'm sorry to disappoint you! I'm the prop man. Assistant!

MOS: Why did you lie to me?

GREGG: Because . . ! (HE PAUSES) Sometimes it's easier.

MOS: You don't have anything to do with Ingrid Bergman?

GREGG: Sure! It's just . . . She treats me like the shit on your shoe! But . . . as the assistant prop man, I do give her things. Can we keep this between ourselves?

YOUNG MOS: What do you give her?

GREGG: The tools of her trade? For instance: the passport, she gives the Russian Commissar on the train as she approaches the Chinese border at the beginning of the movie; the bible, she reads above the grave of little Burt Kwouk towards the end. That's all me.

MOS: You give her things she could take herself?

GREGG: She's a film star. And anyway, it's my speciality! 'The Robe', 'fifty three? That guy; that Marcellus Gallio? I was two steps behind him for the best part of two months. I was in charge of that very garment. Yessir, the cloth of our Lord and saviour was my personal responsibility. I saved that young actor's life on more than one occasion!

MOS: (FORLORNLY) You couldn't save my father.

GREGG: (AFTER SOME CONSIDERATION) I wasn't even here when your father died!

THE LIGHT FADES SLOWLY.
A NEW LIGHT COMES UP ON OLD MOS.

OLD MOS: No different after all perhaps
A bit of a liar, like everybody else
Nothing wrong with it when you're a boy; it makes the world go round
Alwyn Fedw lied for most of his young life
But once a man, his lies could not save him from drowning in the bottomless pool; he couldn't lie himself out of the water
My father could not lie, hurtling down Clogwyn Mawr, grabbing at the empty air – having done so cheerfully six months earlier, as the three English strode to their fate

'Safe as houses!' . . . he proclaimed
'Carry on!'
Bla-bla-bla; bla-bla-bla . . . they carried on
Down the road in their silly knickerbockers
A laugh, as they wished my father well, 'Clogwyn Mawr' sounding like double-Dutch, or Dick Barton on the wireless
Bla-bla-bla.
(PAUSE)
Was it one long 'bla' as they fell, foolishly roped together?
Did my father think 'serves you right' as he counted the bodies?
Did he, I wonder, say 'there, but for the grace of God go I' in his own tongue?
Little knowing that God's grace would cease before the year was out.

THE LIGHT FADES.

THE LIGHT COMES UP. GWYNETH AND YOUNG MOS STAND SIDE BY SIDE, LOOKING STRAIGHT AHEAD. WITH THE LIGHT COMES THE START OF A TERRIBLE STORM: GALE FORCE WINDS; RAIN; THUNDER AND LIGHTNING. GWYNETH PULLS OUT THE PORNOGRAPHIC MAGAZINE FROM HER COAT POCKET AND FLICKS FROM PAGE TO PAGE. SHE BECOMES TOTALLY ENGROSSED, IF NOT A LITTLE EXCITED, WHILE ALL THE WHILE THE STORM RAGES AND INTENSIFIES AROUND HER, REACHING A TERRIBLE CLIMAX AS GWYNETH TEARS AND RIPS THE MAGAZINE INTO PIECES. YOUNG MOS REMAINS MOTIONLESS THROUGHOUT.
THE LIGHT FADES.

THE LIGHT COMES UP ON GREGG. AGAIN, HE IS HUNGOVER, ONLY MORE SO. IN HIS HANDS, SOME DOCUMENTS: A FORM; AN UNEMPLOYMENT CARD.

GREGG: Screw you! Your loss!

GWYNETH APPEARS. GREGG HURRIEDLY PUTS THE DOCUMENTS AWAY. GWYNETH LOOKS RAGGED AND DESPERATE – NO CAP, JUST A MESS OF MATTED, WET HAIR FALLING OVER HER SHOULDERS. SHE AVOIDS GREGG'S EYES; SHE IS ASHAMED TO BE THERE, BUT HAS NO CHOICE.

GREGG: 'Didn't expect to see you.

SILENCE.

GREGG: Some storm, huh!

GWYNETH: 'Used to them.

BUT THE TENSION IN HER IS ALMOST TANGIBLE.

GWYNETH: I've brought you this . . !

SHE REVEALS A PACKAGE.

GWYNETH: A dozen eggs and a pint of milk. One and three for the eggs, seven pence for the milk, making one and ten in all. Oh, there's butter too – cheap and for nothing.

GREGG: Has it got my name on it?

GWYNETH: 'You have the money now?

GREGG: Uh . . . no . . .

GWYNETH: But I must have it today! I must have money this very minute! Don't you get paid on this wonderful film?

GREGG: (HE FALTERS BEFORE REGAINING CONFIDENCE) Sure I get paid!

GWYNETH: Well what about paying me!

GREGG: I could get it to you by tomorrow?

GWYNETH: Tomorrow, indeed! Tomorrow is a hundred miles away when there's no food in your belly!

GREGG: I'm sorry, that's the best I can do!

PAUSE.

GWYNETH: What about the film; do they need more people? I have my jeep, and I'm a good driver!

GREGG: Well, maybe they do, maybe they don't. It's a bit late in the day, that's the truth! 'Should've struck while the iron was hot!

GWYNETH: Can you help me; have a word; get me an introduction?

GREGG CONSIDERS. HE SEES A WINDOW OF OPPORTUNITY.

GWYNETH: Have you lost your tongue? I doubt it! Can you help me, or am I on my own?

GREGG: Depends how desperate the situation is. I'd have to use all of my influence, and that's a fact! Depends . . . how badly you want it, Gwyneth.

GWYNETH: I allowed the fairies into my eyes, to whisper nonsense in my ears. I was looking at the stars, and not at the earth beneath my feet. Six cattle drowned; thirty sheep; most of the harvest like the hair on my head; the roof at the back of the house, and on the big barn blown away, never to return.

GREGG: 'Sounds mighty desperate to me.

GWYNETH: (IT ISN'T EASY FOR HER) Dinner . . . or something, you said; although, we have dinner, dinner time, not at night. That's supper. And I suppose you did mean . . . at night. Is that American?

GREGG NOW KNOWS FOR SURE WHAT'S ON OFFER.

GREGG: We sure could discuss what's possible.

GWYNETH: I don't want to put you in a difficult situation!

GREGG: It's you who's in a difficult situation, Gwyneth, if I may say so.

GREGG GETS PHYSICALLY CLOSE TO HER.

GREGG: Look – we don't have to wait for night. You're in a difficult situation, why prolong the agony? You could check in right now. We'll have you fixed in no time.

PAUSE.

GWYNETH: That . . . magazine: I'm sorry I made such a fuss. I wasn't sorry at the time of course, because of Mos. That kind of thing is not for children.

GREGG: Absolutely not.

HE SLOWLY SWEEPS THE HAIR AWAY FROM HER FACE, AS THE LIGHT FADES.

THE LIGHT COMES UP. YOUNG MOS SITS ON HIS HEELS, WAITING. HE GETS TO HIS FEET, AS GWYNETH APPROACHES. SHE IS RAGGED AND DISTRAUGHT. SHE HURRIES TO YOUNG MOS AND EMBRACES HIM; SHE HOLDS ON TIGHT, SOBBING UNASHAMEDLY. THE LIGHT FADES.

THE LIGHT COMES UP. GREGG IS SWIGGING FROM A HALF-BOTTLE OF WHISKEY. FOR ONCE HE IS HAPPY AND MORE THAN A LITTLE PLEASED WITH HIMSELF. YOUNG MOS APPEARS, PURPOSEFULLY AND AGGRESSIVELY. HE IS WEARING HIS MOTHER'S LONG COAT AND CAP; HE IS BRANDISHING THE 12-BORE SHOTGUN. ALL IN ALL, A RATHER ALARMING SIGHT. GREGG IS ON HIS GUARD IMMEDIATELY.

GREGG: Mos! Hi there, buddy . . !

YOUNG MOS: I'm not your 'buddy'!

GREGG: No? Say, what 'you doin' in your mom's clothes? Is that her gun you've got there . . ? 'Couldn't you find your cowboy outfit!

YOUNG MOS: My father's clothes!

GREGG: Oh!

YOUNG MOS: My father's gun!

GREGG: Right. So . . . 'you looking for foxes? 'Ain't seen none today!

YOUNG MOS: I'm looking for you!

GREGG: You are? Well, here I am! (HE PAUSES; HE KNOWS IT IS SERIOUS) Just . . . tell me what's wrong. How is your mom, by the way?

YOUNG MOS: What have you done to her!

GREGG: When!

YOUNG MOS: You took her to the cottage and locked the door! She came out crying!

GREGG: 'She tell you that? She stepped in of her own accord. It was a mutual thing.

YOUNG MOS: Did you . . . fuck my mother?

GREGG IS TAKEN ABACK BY THIS STARK QUESTION.

YOUNG MOS: I know what it means!

GREGG: No . . !

YOUNG MOS: (HOPEFULLY) You didn't then . . ?

GREGG: You don't know what it means! Knowing the words doesn't always give you meaning! You may have seen the animals, Mos: dog fucking dog; rabbit fucking rabbit; hen fucking . . ! Do hens fuck, or is it mailed?

YOUNG MOS: Did you fuck **her** . . . like an animal?

YOUNG MOS TIGHTENS HIS GRIP ON THE 12-BORE. GREGG IS NERVOUS.

GREGG: Wait! Wait a minute. Lemme show you something.

HE OPENS UP HIS RUCKSACK AND RUMMAGES INSIDE.

YOUNG MOS: What are you doing?

GREGG: Lemme show you this!

HE PULLS OUT A JAPANESE HANDGUN. HE POINTS IT IN THE GENERAL DIRECTION OF YOUNG MOS (WHO BACKS OFF, STARTLED).

YOUNG MOS: *Ffwcin hel!* (Fucking hell!)

GREGG: Would that be 'fucking hell'? Yeah, that's right! Fuck **in** hell, even! But then, you'd know about all that, wouldn't you? Fucking?

YOUNG MOS: What . . . is it?

GREGG: A gun, that's seen some pretty choice action I can tell you!

YOUNG MOS: I've got a bigger gun!

GREGG: And two shots at a time! You'd have to re-load, amigo! Or maybe you could do the job with just the two? Why not give it a try!

HE AIMS HIS GUN DIRECTLY AT YOUNG MOS.

GREGG: You'd be dead before you could say 'Ingrid Bergman'.

YOUNG MOS RELAXES HIS GRIP ON THE 12-BORE. GREGG LOWERS THE HANDGUN.

GREGG: We can be friends. Just the two of us! Pretty and Charlie, right? Who needs women! They just get in the way, don't they? 'Slow everything down! I mean, name me one good Western where the woman plays a significant role?

MOS: Calamity Jane?

GREGG: Think John Wayne; think 'hero'! When did he ever mess around with women?

THE LIGHT FADES ON GREGG AND YOUNG MOS. THE LIGHT COMES UP ON OLD MOS.

OLD MOS: *Help me . . . he used to say*
Give me your trembling hand
Push it in there, into the warm and wet; but it where baby lambs come from
No . . . I used to say: *that's where shit comes from.*
Let me go; the sun's a-setting and the wagon train's a-waiting
It's a long trail to California and gold
Let me free into my own escape
Let me be, and banish the cruel laughter of Wil Myshrwms and Harry Gwastadanas from my head
Witnesses to my horror
(PAUSE)
Wil Myshrwms did not laugh much, staring at the 'beware of smoking' poster, as the kindly nurse told him 'too late, Wil Bach, too late'.
Nor did Harry Gwastadanas cackle, as both horns of Uncle Ben's prize Aberdeen bull tore into his lower belly.
(HE SMILES FAINTLY)
The witnesses . . . are always condemned.

THE LIGHT FADES ON OLD MOS. THE LIGHT COMES UP. GWYNETH FINDS GREGG. THERE IS A SILENCE BETWEEN THEM TO START WITH.

GREGG: 'Saw Mos. 'He tell you?

GWYNETH: Any news? When do I start?

GREGG: Start . . ?

GWYNETH: A woman with jeep and petrol, you said. When . . ?

GREGG: Oh! That; listen . . .

GWYNETH: Guto Garej . . ! He's the man who keeps the garage in the village – he says he won't ask for money until the end of the month. If I can start before then . . !

GREGG: No!

GWYNETH: What do you mean 'no'? Don't tell me 'no'! Tell me when to start!

GREGG: Not at all!

GWYNETH: Not at all! Not at all!

GREGG: You left it too late! You should've struck while the iron was hot! Not so easy, now that everything's snapped up . . .

GWYNETH: Easy! You say 'easy'! You found it very easy to claw your way into my insides! Ten hands you had, if I remember rightly! Don't talk 'easy' with me! It's your turn to give now, after all I gave you!

GREGG: It was a gift?

GWYNETH: It was business! We . . . had a business arrangement. You must keep your side of the bargain.

GREGG: I tell you I can't!

GWYNETH: But it was business! And business is business, *chwadal* (according to) Dafydd Ellis! I've dipped my toe in the water; I've made my cross; now I'm waiting for an introduction.

GREGG: Is that all is was . . ? All that . . ?

GWYNETH:	Yes! It mustn't become anything else! With my dead husband only a wish away . . !
GREGG:	So . . . who did you imagine me to be, Gwyneth?
GWYNETH:	I did not imagine: that particular star died a long time ago. It was business. (SHE PAUSES) Of course . . . you cannot conduct that kind of business entirely without consequences. When a pig's throat is cut, yes, there is bacon; yes, there is food on the table, all winter long; yes, it's very necessary – but there is also blood.
GREGG:	Is that . . . why the 'words' came?
GWYNETH:	There were no words.
GREGG:	Sure there was! Come on, tell me! I don't . . . 'speak the spoke', remember?

GWYNETH STAYS STILL AND SILENT.

GREGG:	Were they for me, Gwyneth – or Ailyn (Alun)?
GWYNETH:	Are you going to help me, or are you not?
GREGG:	(AFTER SOME CONSIDERATION) Lemme help you here on the farm . . !
GWYNETH:	Don't be ridiculous!
GREGG:	Why not!
GWYNETH:	Just look at those putty-white hands!
GREGG:	I had **ten** hands a while ago! Lemme try!

GWYNETH: Doing what . . ! *Argol hedd* (goodness me!), you have no idea! Could you . . . could you work a pick and shovel for six hours at a time? Swing a . . . a *pladur* (scythe) from sunrise to sunset without minding your bleeding hands? Could you climb to the top of Llechwedd Ganol without breaking sweat? (SHE PAUSES) Walk three miles to Caersalem shop in knee-deep snow; walk all the way back lugging a sack of potatoes. (NOW SHE FONDLY REMEMBERS) Ride Sandy at a terrible gallop along the quarry top, the bottomless pit just a careless inch to your right, and Mr. Fawcett and Peter from the Wirral looking on with their mouths as open as Gwenllian's cave! Oh, the sun never went down that day! (SHE PAUSES) Well, could you?

GREGG: Yes! All of that, and more! (HE PAUSES) Maybe; maybe not. That's not the point! In the end, it wouldn't matter. I'd be . . . helping you.

THEIR EYES LOCK. AT THIS MOMENT IN TIME, GWYNETH IS MILDLY TEMPTED AND GREGG IS MILDLY HOPEFUL.

OLD MOS: Help me . . . he used to say. Give me your trembling hand . . .

THE LIGHT COMES UP. YOUNG MOS, IN ORDINARY CLOTHES, COMES ACROSS GREGG, FORLORNLY SWIGGING FROM A HALF-BOTTLE OF WHISKEY.

GREGG: Howdy, stranger! 'Missed you, these last few weeks. But then, I've been kinda busy. What with the Japs closing in an' all . . !

YOUNG MOS: And Mr. Donat dead.

GREGG: That's right!

GREGG PAUSES; HE RECALLS AND CONSIDERS YOUNG MOS'S LAST REMARK.

GREGG: Excuse me? What's that you just said?

YOUNG MOS: There must be plenty to do, now that he's gone.

GREGG: Robert Donat is dead? (HE RECOVERS) I know, isn't it terrible! And so sudden . . !

YOUNG MOS: They say he was nice. Very tall and nice. Of course, he won't be dead when I see him next. He won't be dead in the pictures.

GREGG: How . . . d'you know all of this?

YOUNG MOS: Are you going to the funeral?

GREGG: 'Read it in that 'Weekly News' of yours, I bet!

YOUNG MOS: He only died yesterday!

GREGG: Yesterday? Sure, it was on the cards, I guess. Everybody realised he was mighty ill, Mos! Who told you about Donat . . . uh . . . Robert?

YOUNG MOS: Mr. Mark Robson himself.

GREGG: What . . . you've been down there? Talking to Mark? I don't believe that, you're having me on! Y'know . . . security and the like, it's so tight as a rule.

YOUNG MOS: 'Talked to Ingrid Bergman too!

GREGG: You don't say!

YOUNG MOS: (HE BECOMES RATHER DESPONDENT) Two minutes. We talked for two minutes. Not much to say. Talked funny. Had a pimple on her chin. And she was smoking! 'Never seen a woman smoking before. 'Seen a woman pissing in a field, but never smoking.

GREGG: That's too bad. Did you . . . skip school? You wouldn't want Gwyneth to hear about that, Mos! Look, I'll tell you what, let's keep this between ourselves, huh?

YOUNG MOS JUST STARES AT HIM.

GREGG: What . . !

YOUNG MOS: You are such a liar; a bigger liar than Alwyn Fedw, and he's the biggest liar in the world!

GREGG: (RATHER HELPLESSLY) Yeah?

YOUNG MOS: My mother took me there. They gave her work.

GREGG: Is that right? Well, that's swell! Hey . . . listen, pal – I'm sorry, O.K.? I didn't want to disappoint you! And I tried . . ! I begged them! But it was always 'come back tomorrow'; 'maybe next week'!

YOUNG MOS: Liar! You said you were the assistant director, but you're not. You said you were the prop man, but that's a lie too! You're no more the prop man than the hole of my arse! Not any more!

GREGG: O.K. – so now you know. We . . . had a slight difference of opinion shall we say, and I could compromise my professional integrity no longer. Man, I had to walk!

MOS: Getting drunk; getting thrown out and banned from the Goat Hotel; picking on the **real** assistant director, nice Mr. Middlemas, and giving him a nasty black eye! Everybody knows.

GREGG: (WITHOUT ENTHUSIASM) Fuck you.

A PAUSE. BOTH ARE A LITTLE DESPONDENT.

GREGG: How's Gwyneth?

YOUNG MOS: Mr. Box gave her a bottle of wine on her very first day! From France, he said, nothing like the blueberry I'm allowed when I'm feeling bad. Mr. John Box, he's American, and a very important person. He told me to call him 'John', not 'Mr. Box'. I like that. It's different. (HE PAUSES) She drank the wine; she didn't have tea that day. She started singing. And then she cried.

GREGG: 'She have anything to say about me?

MOS LOOKS AWAY.

GREGG: 'She have anything to say about me, Mos!

THE LIGHT FADES. THE LIGHT COMES UP ON OLD MOS.

OLD MOS: *Come home . . . I said*
People will talk
The piano's out of tune this last hour, and Tom and Bobby are long gone, your only audience being the sleeping barman, and the mad woman from the Polish camp who once exposed herself to Dewi, the simpleton – remember?
(PAUSE)
Remember the rules, handed down from generation to generation:

> Man drinks; woman cooks
> Man fights, woman takes care of the wounded
> Man hurts; woman loves
> Father, once in a blue moon, most welcome: traditional; seasonal; encouraged; controlled
> Part of the fabric; tolerated.
> Come home to tea and toast, and leave the fire-water behind
> Come home, [before the fat dollar captures you forever].

THE LIGHT FADES ON OLD MOS.

THE LIGHT COMES UP ON GWYNETH. SHE IS DRINKING FROM A BOTTLE OF WINE, AND RATHER DRUNK. SHE RUBS HER BELLY ONCE OR TWICE, MAKING IT PLAIN TO THE AUDIENCE THAT SHE IS PREGNANT.

GWYNETH: (LONGINGLY) *'Mae mam wedi madal y tŷ ers y bore*
(My mother has left the house since morning)
A mynd i bregethu toes neb wyr i ble
(She's gone a preaching, God only knows where)
Bydd miloedd o bobl yn gwrando a gweiddi
(Thousands of people will listen and cheer)
A phawb am y gora yn gweiddi hwre'
(And everyone loudly proclaiming 'hurrah')

GREGG COMES INTO VIEW (WITH RUCKSACK). HE LISTENS TO THE REST UNSEEN.

GWYNETH: *'R wy'n siwr o gael drwg gan fy mam – o be' wnai!*
(My mother will punish me, what shall I do!)
A helynt o achos y jam – o be' wnai!
(A fracas because of the jam, what shall I do!)
A'r hen debot tsieni, a'i big wedi torri
(The old china teapot, its beak it is broken)
Bydd mam yn gynddeiriog pan welith hi'r lle'!
(My mother'll be furious when she sees the place!)

GREGG: Tell me the meaning.

GWYNETH: *Arclwy!* (Goodness!) Look who's here: the Indian himself! Or half Indian, whatever you are . . !

GREGG: Quarter. But you know that's bullshit.

GWYNETH: Bull-shit! Yes, a very good description!

A PAUSE.

GREGG: 'Heard you got lucky.

GWYNETH: No thanks to you.

GREGG: 'Guess not.

GWYNETH: I got . . . 'lucky' as you say . . ! . . . because I went down there and put my stonding out for all to see! Mr. John Box – John – liked what he saw and gave me honest employment there and then! Nothing to do with luck.

GREGG: 'Doesn't surprise me. Had I been in Mr. John Box's position, I'd have done the same.

GWYNETH: But you're not, are you? Although . . . I believed you for a while.

GREGG: I didn't mean to harm you.

GWYNETH: You tricked me!

GREGG: I did in a way!

GWYNETH: In every way!

GREGG: 'Least you're working now!

GWYNETH: (PROUDLY) I had to take John around on my very first day! He's the director of the art. American, of course.

GREGG: So . . . what became of the sun, the moon and the seasons?

GWYNETH: What . . ?

GREGG: You sure as hell weren't gonna be dictated to by a bunch of outsiders!

GWYNETH: Are you deaf, dumb . . . and blind? Don't you realise my situation? This is manna from heaven, no less! (SHE SWIGS FROM THE BOTTLE OF WINE; SHE GOES ON PROUDLY) I had eleven Chinese inside me the other day! Eight in the back and three in the front! Is it a record? Jim Newcome was most impressed!

GREGG: You'll have 'em inside your house, some day.

GWYNETH: The Chinese?

GREGG: Rulers of the universe. 'Says so in the good book.

GWYNETH: You don't believe in the good book!

GREGG: I believe that.

GWYNETH: About the Chinese?

GREGG: Chinese; Koreans; Japs! Especially the Japs.

GWYNETH: Don't be ridiculous! If we didn't have the Chinese – or Japanese for that matter – I wouldn't be driving the jeep for Mr. John Box! Ingrid Bergman would be fighting thin air! Don't be . . . **fucking** ridiculous!

SHE MAKES A DELIBERATE 'SHOW' OF THE WORD 'FUCKING', BUT IT ISN'T SECOND NATURE.

GREGG: Christ, don't! Don't . . . say that.

GWYNETH: Film people, they say it all the time. (FONDLY) Especially Tom and Bobby on the chuck wagon! It's 'fuck this', 'fuck that' every other word!

GREGG: That's not very clever, Gwyneth; a young mother like you.

GWYNETH: (WITH IRONY) Young mother! Yes, that's a laugh! What is it? You want me to be a nice little woman for ever I suppose? Sitting by the fire, waiting. Warm food on the table; warm bed.

GREGG: Don't disappoint me.

GWYNETH: (SOFTLY) 'Mae mam wedi madal . . . y tŷ ers y bore A mynd i bregethu . . . toes neb wyr i ble . . .'

GREGG: Explain the words.

GWYNETH: Nothing to explain. It's just a silly song my mother used to sing – about a good woman . . . or a bad woman, depending on your point of view; a religious woman . . . or a woman selling herself. (SHE PAUSES)
I remember . . ! . . . sitting here with my mother when I was a young girl, in exactly the same spot as we are now. I was eight years old, and she told me, completely out of the blue as it were: 'I won't be here forever'.
'I won't be here forever'? What a terrible thing to say to a slip of a girl. We all have to die, yes. Not at eight years of age. That's how I felt, the life draining out of me, there and then. I made my pillow into an extra-deep rabbit's hutch that night, and pushed my head right inside as far as it would go.

GREGG: (A LITTLE LOST) Can I hold you?

GWYNETH: (MID-ATLANTIC TWANG OF SORTS) Gee, this is a wunnerful country! (SHE LAUGHS) Gee . . ! . . . this is a wunnerful country! I'm saying 'wonderful', do you understand?

GREGG: 'Sure do. 'Sure is swell.

GWYNETH: Swell! Mark; Mark Robson, he says it all the time! So does Jim Newcome! Do you know Jim? Have you met him? 'Hi, Gwyneth'! he says, several times a day. 'See ya later'! – he says that too. He means 'goodbye, see you tomorrow'. 'Later' to me, you see, is ten or fifteen minutes, half an hour at the most. When Mos asks for a boiled sweet from the Coronation canister on the top of the dresser, and I say 'later', it's exactly that – later – not the next day! So funny! Do you know Jim? You must have come across him in the lounge bar at the Goat Hotel. He's always there.

GREGG: I'm banned.

GWYNETH: He's always there . . !

GREGG: 'Full of Japs. 'Can't get served.

GWYNETH: Chinese! Chinese, what's the matter with you!

GREGG: Sure.

GWYNETH: Where do you live . . !

GREGG: That's a tough one.

PAUSE.

GWYNETH: I had a drink with Mr. Mark Robson himself the other day . . ! Very swank! I was with John and Jim to tell you the honest truth, but Mark was about too – up in his room, entertaining Miss Bergman some say. I had four glasses altogether! I couldn't stop talking for the whole hour I was there! But I don't remember half of what I said! Anyway, I don't think they minded; they were all laughing, anyway! And driving the jeep on the road home? Don't ask! Off I went – *igam-ogam* – that's from side to side to you – and when I came speeding down Cwm Dyli pass, I nearly missed the turning and went over!

GREGG: 'Shame the Japs weren't still inside. 'Could've taken some of 'em with you, Gwyneth.

GWYNETH: Chinese! They're Chinese, what's the fucking matter with you!

GREGG: Don't use that language!

GWYNETH: It's **your** language!

A PAUSE. BOTH ARE QUITE EMOTIONAL.

GREGG: (FINALLY) Please . . . let me help you; Mos, too. Give me this chance.

GWYNETH: You can't help me! You don't work with the 'Sixth Happiness'; you don't like the Chinese; and you don't drink in the lounge bar at the Goat Hotel with John and Jim . . !

YOUNG MOS COMES INTO VIEW.

YOUNG MOS: *Ydach chi'n dwad adra rwan?* (Are you coming home now?)

GWYNETH: Have you forgotten your manners all of a sudden? We do have company, you know!

YOUNG MOS: *Ydach chi'n dwad adra, mam!* (Are you coming home, mam!)

GWYNETH: What is wrong with you . . ! Are you totally ignorant? Say something we can all understand, or don't say anything at all!

GREGG: No matter, Gwyneth.

GWYNETH: Hoping to become a world-famous film star, *wir!* (indeed!). Not if you carry on like this!

GREGG: He can speak what he likes; it's no big deal.

GWYNETH: But what's the **point!** If people don't understand you . . . what is the point? Where would **I** be . . . if Jim Newcome . . . or Mark . . . or even Ingrid herself couldn't understand what I'm saying! [Why, only the other day John Box asked my advice about a dead sheep he'd bought off Gwilym *Bwtsiar* (Butcher) to decorate the bandits' camp! In this warm weather it had naturally started to smell a bit; I told him to gut it and throw away the insides. Now then, would I have been able to tell him that if I couldn't speak properly?] Would I be driving my jeep for five English pounds a day, and drinking in the lounge bar of the Goat Hotel if I spoke *rwtsh* (rubbish)?!

GREGG: You've had enough. (WINE)

GWYNETH: What did you say?

YOUNG MOS: You're making a fool of yourself!

GWYNETH: Oh, he can speak it! Listen! It's **you** . . ! . . . who's the fool!
You, and your father before you!

YOUNG MOS: *Peidiwch!* (Don't!)

GWYNETH: Don't you '*peidiwch*' me! 'Wouldn't speak! He wouldn't speak the spoke when it mattered! I mean, everybody goes to the pictures, don't they? Everybody understands! But no, not him. Visitors . . ! . . . turning away, because he wouldn't answer in a common tongue when they asked for milk and butter! And who knows . . ! . . . he might be still with us today, if only . . ! (SHE PAUSES)
[Broken on those rocks, perhaps still alive for all we know, he could have saved himself by calling out in the proper way!

GREGG: 'Help' is 'help' all over, ain't it?]

YOUNG MOS MAKES TO LEAVE.

GWYNETH: And where do you think you're going? Come back this minute!

YOUNG MOS IGNORES HER. GWYNETH RESTRAINS HIM PHYSICALLY.

GWYNETH: *Gwranda arna'i pan 'dw i'n siarad efo chdi'r llymbar! 'D'wyt ti ddim wedi mynd rhy hen i gael cweir!*
(Listen to me when I'm talking to you! You're not too old for a good beating!)

SHE STARTS WALLOPING HIM, ALTHOUGH FEW OF THE BLOWS ACTUALLY MAKE CONTACT. YOUNG MOS DOESN'T RESIST, OR FIGHT BACK.

GREGG: No . . . don't. Gwyneth, no! Leave the kid alone!

YOUNG MOS: I'm not a kid!

GREGG: Leave him alone, for crying out loud!

GREGG PHYSICALLY SEPARATES GWYNETH FROM YOUNG MOS.

GREGG: [Whatever it is, don't take it out on him!]

A MOMENT, AS GWYNETH SQUARES UP TO GREGG AGGRESSIVELY.
THEN IT ALL CRUMBLES, AND SHE HURRIES AWAY.

GREGG: Holy Mother of fucking Jesus . . !

HE RUMMAGES IN HIS RUCKSACK, TAKES OUT A FULL BOTTLE OF WHISKEY AND UNAPOLOGETICALLY DRINKS FROM IT DEEP.

YOUNG MOS: I don't think he likes being called that.

GREGG: Who . . ? What!

YOUNG MOS: Jesus. 'Fucking Jesus': you don't hear it said much around here.

PAUSE

YOUNG MOS: You OK?

GREGG: ['She hurt you?] It's all going to be OK. 'Done really well! 'Should be proud of her.

YOUNG MOS: Is 'doing well' . . . leaving the cows unmilked for hours at a time; forgetting to close the *bompren* (gate), and letting sheep wander into the road so that Mr. Gresham's big Vellocet motorbike kills three in one go?

GREGG: I missed that.

YOUNG MOS: Putting marmalade on my bread and butter, instead of syrup. I hate marmalade.

GREGG: Listen . . ! All of that, it'll fall back into place once this thing is over; once the circus moves on.

SILENCE.

YOUNG MOS: Are you . . . moving on?

GREGG: Would you like me to stay? 'Biggest liar in the whole darn world, remember!

YOUNG MOS: No, that's Alwyn Fedw.

GREGG: You mean to say he's bigger than me?

AN EXCHANGE OF SMILES.

GREGG: Your mom needs help, that's her problem: on the farm; in life. Someone to look out for her.

YOUNG MOS: She's got me!

GREGG: You were hell bent on becoming a film star, five minutes ago!

YOUNG MOS: (RATHER DESPONDENTLY) Like a bird, flying to the top of Moel Druman mountain once every hundred years; pecking a small piece away until there's nothing left . . .

GREGG: Maybe I could help you . . ! Maybe . . . just maybe . . . I could get you an introduction. Not here, not now, but two or three years down the line, say! I'm talking Hollywood, Mos!

YOUNG MOS: You're talking rubbish.

GREGG: No! We could hit the trail together, you and I; head out west; make our fortune. Hey, Charlie . . ! Saddle up!

YOUNG MOS: Sandy doesn't wear a saddle; she's a working horse.

GREGG: 'Still don't trust me, huh?

GREGG GOES INTO HIS RUCKSACK AND GETS OUT THE JAPANESE HANDGUN.

GREGG: Here; take it.

YOUNG MOS STANDS BACK.

GREGG: Take it; go on, have a feel.

GINGERLY, MOS TAKES THE GUN.

YOUNG MOS: Has it . . . ever been used?

GREGG: (EASILY) Sure. Many times. 'Killed two, in open combat. All legal.

YOUNG MOS: You shot . . . two people?

GREGG: Before they could shoot me.

YOUNG MOS: *Esgob!* (Wow!)

GREGG: Have it.

YOUNG MOS: What . . ?

GREGG: It's yours: a token of my friendship, Mos. Whatever happens, we'll always be brothers.

YOUNG MOS STARES AT THE GUN. IT'S THE HAPPIEST MOMENT OF HIS LIFE SO FAR.

YOUNG MOS: To keep . . ?

GREGG: For ever and ever, Amen.

YOUNG MOS: *Esgob!* (Wow!) This is . . . like getting long trousers for the first time! I'll never be unhappy again! It's like . . . nothing I know. (HE CARESSES THE GUN) It's like . . .

OLD MOS: Dangling my feet in six inches of water, with Marcia Wheeler by my side, in her smooth, brown skin and pony tail! Talking about the big fire on Mynydd Bach – started deliberately, some say!
[HE BECOMES ENGROSSED IN HIS MEMORIES, ALL THE WHILE CARESSING THE GUN] Sitting next to her, pushing my hand down her shorts. (HE PAUSES) Sitting still, with the birds and water getting louder and louder, thinking that nothing else in the whole world would matter again – not even the atom bomb.

GREGG: So what happened?

YOUNG MOS: That *ffwcin* (fucking) Alwyn Fedw came to spoil the party, and Marcia got up and went. I was very angry with Alwyn at first, but then we had a great game of 'Charlie and Pretty' – the best ever.

THE LIGHT FADES ON YOUNG MOS AND GREGG. A LIGHT COMES UP ON OLD MOS.

OLD MOS: *Do you have a mountain . . .* she asked
In her *pwdin plwm* (plum pudding) voice
A shelter; a grassy corner, gentle on my bare behind
Do you have transport, there and back?
Rings are cheap at Criciath fair
Silly things from Surrey, cheaper

Bla-bla-bla.
(PAUSE)
Hurry . . . I said
The nights are drawing in, and my *lob sgows* is getting cold
Searching eyes are waiting at the kitchen door
Ten, twenty strokes at the most, and the chasing and the longing over, and Charlie and Pretty can return to indian country and safety.
(PAUSE)
Don't write
Go a different route, next summer
Blackpool's nice.

THE LIGHT FADES ON OLD MOS.

THE LIGHT COMES UP. WE FIND GWYNETH, LOOKING RATHER WILD AND DISTRAUGHT.

GWYNETH: 'Mae mam wedi madal y tŷ ers y bore
(My mother has left the house since morning)
'A mynd i . . . bregethu . . . toes neb wyr i ble'
(She's gone . . . a-preaching . . . God only knows where).

SHE PAUSES; SHE SLIPS INTO THE FOLLOWING ELVIS CLASSIC SOFTLY:

GWYNETH: 'Love me tender . . . love me sweet
Never let me go.'
'You have made my life complete
And I love you so.'
'Love me tender . . . love me true . . .
All my dreams fulfill
For, my darlin' I love you
And I always will . . .'

DURING THE ABOVE, MOS APPEARS, CLUTCHING THE JAPANESE HANDGUN. HE OBSERVES GWYNETH, IN BETWEEN TWO MINDS. THE HANDGUN REPRESENTS HIS FANTASY WORLD, AND A POSSIBLE FUTURE WITH GREGG – WHILE GWYNETH IS THE REALITY OF HIS LIFE.

THE LIGHT FADES.

THE LIGHT COMES UP GWYNETH IS ON HER OWN. GREGG STAGGERS INTO VIEW. HE SEEMS DRUNK, OR EUPHORIC, OR BOTH. GWYNETH IS DISGUSTED AND DISAPPOINTED BY HIS APPEARANCE.

GWYNETH: I wish I could be as sure of the weather as I am of you!

GREGG: D'you wanna hear the good news?

GWYNETH: Let me guess: you don't drink when you're asleep?

GREGG: What's that old English saying about the pot calling the kettle black?

GWYNETH: There's no welcome for you here.

GREGG: D'you wanna hear the good news?

GWYNETH STAYS SILENT.

GREGG: If you don't, I'm leaving. I'm walking right out of your life.

PAUSE

GREGG: For ever, Gwyneth! Never to return.

PAUSE

GREGG: I want to tell you the good news, Gwyneth, but you gotta want to hear it.

GREGG SHAKES HIS HEAD.

GWYNETH: I want to hear it! Satisfied?

GREGG: They gave me my job back.

GWYNETH: A lie, without shame or hesitation!

GREGG: I met John Box in the village; we had a conversation; I'm back on the set as from tomorrow . . .

GWYNETH: Has he taken leave of his senses!

GREGG: Had to celebrate, didn't I?

GWYNETH: Of course! You have to celebrate getting out of bed in the morning!

GREGG: They all came! Mark and John; Newcome and Middlemas; Tom and Bobby – even the Ingrid tore herself from Roberto's loins to be there! All smiles; all forgiven; everybody friends!

GWYNETH: And you think that makes everything alright?

GREGG: I'd thought you'd be happy –

GWYNETH: What do you expect? That madness will soon be gone, and we'll still be left to pick up the pieces . . .

GREGG: What if I stayed?

GWYNETH: (CONTEMPT) And live on the wind . . !

GREGG: Would you want me to?

GWYNETH: That's a stupid question. Ridiculous question . . .

HE SORT OF SLUMPS TO THE GROUND (SEATED). HIS EYES CLOSE MOMENTARILY.

GWYNETH: Don't sleep! Not on my land . . .

SHE CONSIDERS HIM; SHE RELENTS A LITTLE.

GREGG: Mr Gresham: the weird Mr Gresham . . . He's getting old: what's to come is less than what's been, I guess. Said he needed help at the farm.

GWYNETH: You're . . . going to stay?

GREGG: Does that make you happy?

GWYNETH: Happy! Just look at you!

GREGG: Does . . . it . . . make you happy?

SLOWLY, GREGG TOPPLES OVER; HE COMES TO REST FLAT ON HIS BACK; HIS COAT OPENS UP, TO REVEAL A LOT OF BLOOD AND A NASTY WOUND TO HIS SIDE.

GWYNETH: O, Dduw . . ! (Oh, God!) What have you done . . !

SHE RUSHES OVER; SHE LIFTS HIM UPRIGHT AND CRADLES HIM IN HER ARMS.

GWYNETH: You fool! What have you gone and done!

SLOWLY, GREGG OPENS HIS EYES AND MANAGES A SMILE.

GREGG: A guy's gotta do, what a guy's gotta do . . .

GWYNETH: I did not dream of this again! One man's broken body is enough to last a lifetime! Who did this to you?

GREGG: You should see the other guy . . !

GWYNETH: It's not funny!

HE LAUGHS, BUT IT IS PAINFUL.

GREGG: It's not funny . . . no.

GWYNETH: Was there a fight?

GREGG: I can see it, Gwyneth – but they can't.

YOUNG MOS COMES INTO VIEW. GREGG'S APEARANCE ISN'T A COMPLETE SURPRISE TO HIM.

GREGG: Hi, partner . . !

YOUNG MOS: They're looking for you: Wilias Policeman in his big van by the quarry gate; Robaits Policeman at the top of Pengwryd; and Jos Policeman up in Bwlch Batal, just in case.

GREGG: Head him off at the pass.

GWYNETH: (TO MOS) Go home. Put the kettle to boil. Fetch sheets from the airing cupboard – and saddle the horse. *Cer!* (Go!)

MOS GOES. GWYNETH CLINGS TO GREGG. THE LIGHT FADES.

THE LIGHT COMES UP. GREGG, GWYNETH AND YOUNG MOS ARE STANDING IN A ROW, AT THE TOP OF A MOUNTAIN. GREGG IS PATCHED UP NOW, AND IS WEARING THE LONG RAINCOAT AND CAP (ALUN'S) WE'VE SEEN BOTH GWYNETH AND YOUNG MOS WEAR PREVIOUSLY.

GREGG: I . . . see them. Dammit, I can see them all!

YOUNG MOS: Llyn Gwynant; Llyn Dinas; Llyn Llagi; Llyn Coch . . .

GREGG: 'Llyn' . . . is 'lake'.

FOR THE FIRST TIME, HE MANAGES TO MAKE THE 'LL' SOUND.

OLD MOS: Cerrig y Myllt, *bach a mawr* (big and small); Llydaw; Biswail; Clogyn Brith . . .

GREGG: Let's get closer! Come on, let's go!

BUT NOBODY MAKES A MOVE.

YOUNG MOS: If you travel far enough, you'll reach Liverpool.

GREGG: I've heard of that place. Is it West? Get my horse, Charlie – I'm goin' home.

FOR A FEW SECONDS MORE GREGG, GWYNETH AND YOUNG MOS REMAIN IN A ROW, ALL STILL AND SILENT. THE LIGHT CHANGES, ISOLATING THEM. GREGG STEPS OUT OF THE LIGHT AND MELTS AWAY; OLD MOS APPEARS, AND TAKES HIS PLACE BY GWYNETH'S SIDE. GWYNETH STROKES HER BELLY GENTLY WITH HER HAND. SHE SMILES FAINTLY.

OLD MOS: And so they came from the great plain of Wirral, driving the Apache before them into residential homes and mental institutions.
Not a Gresham here, or a Fawcett there, too few to bother with, but many: Dundas; Turner; Roach; Green;

Alancroft and Hewitt.
Passing the time of day with the Breton onion-seller was without worry in comparison; learning the word 'because' in a morning, oblivious to the others waiting in ambush, seems very easy from this distance.
Help me . . . I cried – huddled by the bedside of the last great Apache.
Is it not better to remember the good times and end it all?
Wait . . . she said
Remember our tiny bundle of salvation; our very own half-breed
Hold on to her, and the reason for holding on to your ragged corner of the earth
Where there's young life, there's hope.
Not until the last bird has flown to the top of Moel Druman mountain will it finally be over.
Life's too soon as it is.

And with those precious words from her cracked lips, I devoured the speak she spoke.

DURING THE ABOVE, OLD MOS REACHES OUT WITH HIS HAND, IN THE HOPE GWYNETH WILL TAKE HOLD OF IT. SHE DOESN'T. GWYNETH STEPS OUT OF THE LIGHT AND MELTS AWAY. THIS LEAVES YOUNG MOS AND OLD MOS, SIDE BY SIDE. DURING THE FOLLOWING, YOUNG MOS GRADUALLY STEPS OUT OF THE LIGHT AND MELTS AWAY, LEAVING OLD MOS ON HIS OWN.

ELIN APPEARS, IN MODERN DRESS. SHE IS GWYNETH AND GREGG'S DAUGHTER, AND IS FORTY FIVE YEARS OF AGE. SHE STANDS BY OLD MOS'S SIDE. SHE IS HOLDING A SMALL BUNCH OF WILD FLOWERS. SHE CAREFULLY PLACES THE FLOWERS ON THE FLOOR (AS IF ON A GRAVE). SHE STRAIGHTENS UP, AND WITHOUT FUSS TAKES HOLD OF OLD MOS'S HAND. BOTH START SINGING SOFTLY (AND NOT WITHOUT SOME JOY).

OLD MOS/ELIN:
>'Ma' mam wedi madal . . . y tŷ ers y bore
>A mynd i bregethu toes neb wyr i ble
>Bydd miloedd o bobl yn gwrando a gweiddi
>A phawb am y gora yn gweiddi 'hwre''

AND SO ON. THE LIGHT SLOWLY FADES DURING THE SONG.

END